Domino

Also by Linda Ireland

THEM: The Handy Experience Manual

(with Chris LaVictoire Mahai)

Linda Ireland has been building and developing organizations for more than 20 years. Acting as general manager, line executive, entrepreneur, consultant or board member, she is well-versed in implementing strategic change in a variety of environments.

Linda has led organizations in technology, manufacturing, multi-channel retail, financial products and health services, from chairs that include strategy, brand, product, operations, corporate development and governance.

With a career story so diverse in industry, functional role and organization needs, Linda has been called a "build this or fix that" person, and she has enjoyed every chapter.

She has been co-owner and partner of Aveus since 2002.

AVEUS

Aveus is a global strategy and operational change firm. Working with leaders of organizations from small to large, across the United States, Asia and Europe, in industries where the world is changing how things can or must be done, we thrive on making complex challenges doable.

For Chris and Sue, who helped clear the way.
And for Becky, who helped clear the mist.

Domino

How Customer Experience Can Tip Everything in Your Business toward Better Financial Performance

Linda Ireland

AVEUS
Saint Paul, MN

Printed in the United States of America

Library of Congress Cataloging-in-Publication Data

ISBN NUMBER: 978-0-9819302-1-3

20 0 8 9 4 3 2 7 5

Any how-to book worth the paper on which it is printed requires a purpose: *How to do what?*

This book is about how to define a target customer experience, then use it to create measurable performance reward.

Customer experience is discussed often but rarely defined. Here is my definition:

Customer experience is what happens and how customers feel as they:

- Realize a **need**,
- **Learn** about their options to solve the need,
- **Try** out options,
- **Buy**,
- **Solve** their problem, and
- **Evolve** to another need over time.

Contents

Introduction: The Line of Falling Dominos

Several years ago I taught a roomful of graduate students in the MBA program at the University of St. Thomas in Minnesota. On the first night of the course, my students turned the tables and taught me a valuable lesson about the purpose of every business.

I had given the students a daunting challenge: I told them to imagine that the board of directors of a $600 million publicly traded company had just named them to the job of CEO. After a hearty congratulations, the board had dropped a "think-quick" bombshell:

"The auditorium next door is filled with people from all of your stakeholder groups. There are some current and potential customers, some employees, some shareholders and some members of the communities where we do business. They have asked for a quick five-minute speech from you, and they really just want to know one thing: '*What is the purpose of your business?*'"

After I bolted the door to keep my students from running away, I gave them 20 minutes to collaborate on the five-minute speech the CEO should give. They debated and argued their way to a concise definition of the purpose that would drive daily decisions across their company. I listened in (and ducked to avoid thrown objects).

First I heard: "The purpose of a business is to make a profit. Without a profit, there is no money to hire people or create new products and services or give back to the community or reward shareholders."

Then someone argued: "No, the purpose of our business is to create something truly unique that no one else has. If we do that customers will seek us out, and that will drive revenue.

And revenue will attract great employees who will create great profits, enabling us to give back to our communities."

A whole group of students argued that the purpose of the business is customer satisfaction: "Our purpose must be to delight customers so that we will have sustainable revenue, and we'll figure out how to ensure we are profitable." Someone else argued for providing meaningful jobs to society.

As I listened to their list of "purposes," I started to visualize a line of falling dominos, several of them standing on their edges single file, front to back in a row, poised so that when the first domino is tipped, the whole line falls cleanly in succession, a precise chain reaction of events.

I realized my students were arguing over what should be the front and back dominos. In the back—the measure of success or failure. This is the outcome domino. They decided that for the firm I asked them to lead, the outcome metric is profit (and I agreed). In the front stands the purpose domino—the action domino that drives all the others to fall into place. In the middle, daily decisions and actions that must align with the purpose in order to tip the back domino to win a performance payoff. It was my purpose question that had spurred the debate. That's where things became really interesting.

In a nutshell, the class was arguing about what should be the driver of daily decision making in order to achieve a financial performance reward. If the back domino was profit, and the operating actions of a company were all the dominos in the chain reaction between the front and the back, what would they name that domino that stood at the very front of it all?

At the last moment one of the women said, "What if we matched a problem we could solve well with a big target market of customers who would truly value having the solution? That would drive revenue (because it's a real problem for a big market) and margin (because the solution is valuable). That would attract great employees, who could anticipate more needs to solve well. Solving lots of problems well at good margins will contribute mightily to our ability to give back to the communities where we do business. Customers would be advocates for our brand. And we would have plenty of return for our shareholders."

She turned the room.

She saw a link between the action of solving a problem well for the right target customer (the purpose of a business), and financial performance (the outcome).

Driving home after that class, I reflected on how often I had witnessed business leaders miss that valuable link. I thought about how often I had seen them see it but dismiss it. How some had confused purpose with outcome, declaring "our strategy is to maximize profit" and therefore poorly aligned their operating actions to a purpose that would get and keep customers. I considered other leaders I knew who had somehow used the link to make a profound positive difference for their organizations. And of course, I thought about how often I had missed, dismissed or embraced the link in my own successes and missteps as an executive—one who was trying "customer experience" as the front domino long before it was a common phrase on business bookshelves.

Shortly after that class, our consulting firm, Aveus, completed its first of two rounds of empirical research, in which we studied several companies—across a broad variety of sizes and industries—to define the link between customer experience and performance. From over 1000 leaders across two rounds of research, our findings validated the existence of this link, and prompted us to take a deeper look at those organizations that were doing best at unlocking a performance reward. We identified the factors these high-performing companies had in common.

Excited by our findings, I started thinking about writing a strategy book.

Then over dinner, my business partner Chris and I had an aha moment: A strategy book full of models and case studies may have its place in my future, but what leaders really need is a how-to book. What if I could prove how customer experience can create a performance reward by providing real-life, day-to-day, how-to-execute assistance to the leaders who hunger for it? What if we could offer usable tools and instructions to help companies do something with the knowledge that customer experience can lead to better business performance?

That help is now in your hands. With it, you have the key to unlocking great financial rewards from your customers.

Chapter 1: Reward and Punishment

Is your customer experience making you money?
Is it costing you money?
Do you know?

Customer experience matters. I imagine that you agree since you're reading this page. Perhaps you sponsor or lead customer experience projects in the marketing or service or brand functions in your organization. Your organization may have a "Chief Experience Officer." Maybe you've hired consultants. Regardless of how you define the phrase, customer experience matters to organizations of any size, industry or mission.

I, too, think customer experience matters. In a national research study recently published by my firm, Aveus, we found that nearly two-thirds of leaders say their organizations have a well-understood definition of customer experience. Of those who don't claim an organization-wide understanding of customer experience, nearly a third say they *should* have one. Customer experience is now a common part of our business lexicon; staunch believers might even call it a "movement." Customer experience matters regardless of what your organization does or for whom you do it.

Despite all of our collective assertions that customer experience matters, I meet too few executives who claim a performance payoff for their efforts to excel at it. Some say customer experience is a painful financial drain or, at best, a tradeoff to maximizing profits. Others sheepishly admit they don't know whether their customer experience makes or costs money for their organizations. Some have begun to register meaningful performance wins, but want much, *much* more.

So we have a paradox:

> *Customer experience matters and too few leaders declare their customer experience generates money.*

It is time to dispel the thinking that makes this sad statement true.

The paradox is amazing, really. It is a contemporary expression of the timeless lesson from business school that the true purpose of a business is to get and keep customers. Why, then, do so few leaders say they earn a clear *reward* for understanding that lesson?

I have learned that customers reward or punish a business based on its attention to their point of view. Put another way, organizations earn reward or punishment based on how well they translate customer experience from a popular business phrase into a set of consistent, specific actions that solve their customers' most essential needs.

Your customer experience can generate revenue and profitability, or drain from it. You can win—or win *more*—reward.

Over 25 years as a line manger, executive, consultant and researcher, I've learned that there is a way to use customer experience to reap real performance rewards.

Ask Ezra Ernst. While CEO of the North American division of Swets, a global subscriptions management media company, Ezra and his team defined a target customer experience. Then they used it to build a road map of actions that halted a four-year slide in revenues and improved profitability by 25 percent.

Ask Starbucks' Howard Schultz, whose customer experience-driven actions fueled the company's meteoric rise (as well as its corresponding struggle when focus wandered).

Our recent national research study found further evidence of the link between customer experience and performance. We asked nearly 650 leaders whether their organizations had a commonly understood definition of customer experience. We also asked about performance. We found that twice as many organizations that begin with customer experience exceed revenue and profit targets than those that do not begin with it. (Wow.)

> This unmistakable link between customer experience and profitability strikes me as an unnecessarily well-kept secret. It's really very simple.
>
> *Customer experience matters because it drives performance.*

What is customer experience, really?

For all the talk of why customer experience matters, it is rarely defined in actionable terms. Here is my definition:

Customer experience is what happens and how customers feel as they:

- Realize a **need**,
- **Learn** about their options to solve the need,
- **Try** out options,
- **Buy**,
- **Solve** their problem, and
- **Evolve** to another need over time.

If you put this definition of customer experience in a picture—following the idea of getting and keeping customers—it would look like this:

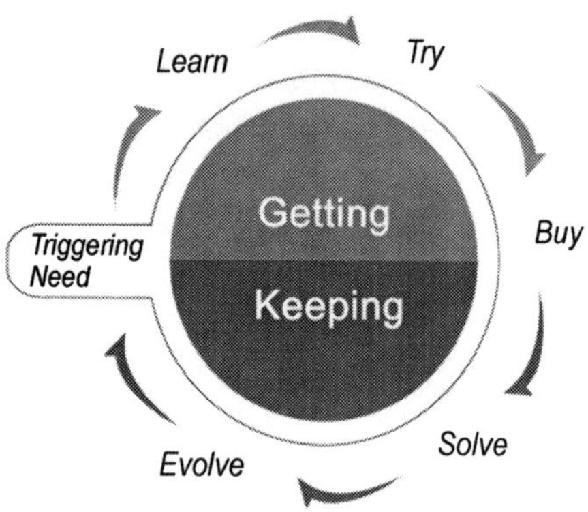

Of course, your organization already has a customer experience. You have had one, in fact, since the day you first had a customer. It may not be the one you planned. It may not be the one you want. From your customers' point of view, it defines you. And whether you manage it or not, it delivers a performance reward or punishment for your organization.

Important facts about your customer experience

Your customer experience has several principles in common with every other customer experience:

- It has the **same form,** no matter what kind of need you solve or profile of customer you serve. Every need, problem or desire is the beginning of an experience, and every experience has the same structure. Every customer—in fact, every *stakeholder* who can or does interact with your company has a need and an experience.

- It is **chronological**. Your organization "touches" your customers many ways. You may process a payment, mail a catalog, hold a live-chat support session and design the next product they will buy. These things may happen concurrently for you, but your customers' experience unfolds one step at a time.

- It includes both **tangible and intangible elements**. Tangible elements include the product or service itself, the price, the length of your purchase contracts or the number of steps a customer must take to get help. Intangible, or emotional, elements include the music your phone system plays while your customers are on hold or the tone conveyed by your Web site when you explain your return policies.

  Using this book as an example, the tangible elements are the specific words I use, the facts I share, the sturdiness of the paper. Now add the intangible—the way you felt when you saw the cover, the tone you hear in my voice. We can identify the elements separately, but they are meaningless without one another.

- It is **universal** across locations and media. Customers have a single relationship with your company, no matter where they hear about you, buy or get help. Even if a prospect learns about your company through a friend or on YouTube and you had no control over that interaction, it is part of that customer's experience with your firm. Your customer experience encompasses all media—and all interactions.

- It is **cumulative**. Customers remember. Each time they interact with your organization, they write a new chapter to the story they carry in their hearts and minds. This holds true even if your business is transaction-based.

Customer experience is like conversation. Each person speaks, reacting and adding to the facts and tone shared by the one who spoke before. Some conversations happen quickly. Some unfold over years. Every interaction can build or weaken relationships.

Your organization's experience

No full definition of customer experience is complete without including the organization's role, too. After all, for your business, you choose which customers to target. You choose the need you will solve for them. You choose the products and services you offer, the way you differentiate your company, and how you organize and fulfill what you sell. You choose the performance outcome and position in the marketplace you want to achieve.

I have observed that the organizations that perform strongest—in getting and keeping customers and in revenue and profit—create a mutual self interest with their customers. Call it a "you solve my problem well and I give you a reward" shared self interest. (Hopefully it is not a "you don't do anything meaningful for me and I punish you" deal, although those types of relationships do exist.)

So there is a "flip side" to my simple definition of customer experience. I call it your *organization experience.* It is the actions *you* take to:

- **Choose** target customers with a need you can solve,
- **Earn** consideration as they learn about options,
- **Demonstrate** you are best to solve the need,
- **Protect** customers as they buy,
- **Prove** your promise, and
- **Anticipate** their next need.

In a picture, here is your organization's experience:

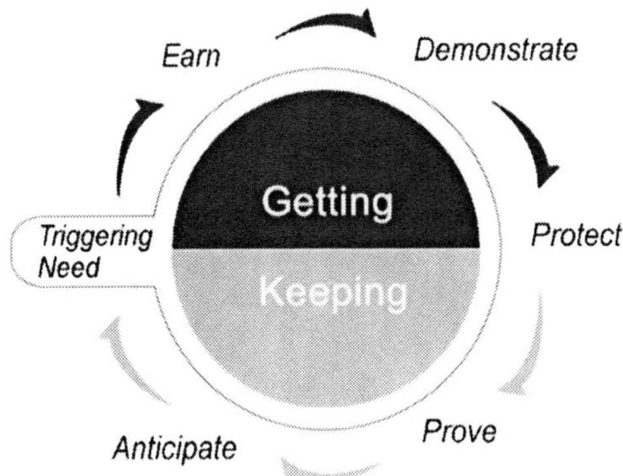

How are you doing?

Let's do a quick exercise to diagnose the effectiveness of your existing customer experience. On the next three pages, you will see a series of questions that canvass the customer experience as I have defined it. On the left side of each page are questions you should answer from the perspective of your ideal customer. (To do it right, answer these not as just *any* customer, but as one of the target customers who holds the best promise of growth and profitability for your organization.) On the right side of the page are questions to answer from your company's perspective.

From your
target customer's
point of view:

Consider: *What is the desire,* ***need*** *or problem that causes you to act for or consider an answer or solution? Is there a frustration, pain or yearning you would like to go away? Given the old adage "People don't buy drills – they buy 1/4 inch holes to build houses," what are you buying?*

From your
organization's
point of view

Assess: What **problem do you solve** for target customers? Why will their lives change if they buy? How does the problem you solve define the size of your target market? Does everyone in your organization focus on solving this problem, or on something else?

Consider: *How do you* ***learn*** *about options? What do you do first in pursuit of a solution? Do you look around to see what others are doing or begin your search independently? What makes an option worthy of consideration? You're looking for a few credible options to consider – creating a real or mental "short list."*

Assess: Are you **earning consideration** from the right prospects for your company? Are you attracting enough of them? Are you getting a sufficient return on investment for your prospecting efforts?

From your
target customer's
point of view:

From your
organization's
point of view

Consider: *How do you test or* ***try the options*** *on your short list? Is it easy to see how each will solve your need? If there are others who influence your decision, how do your options help you engage them? How do you feel as you decide to buy? You're imagining what will happen after the purchase. You are looking for the tangible things that most directly solve your need – and for that "does it feel right" chemistry.*

Assess: Do you **demonstrate how well you can solve** a prospect's need? Do you build differentiation from competitors based on solving your prospect's need, or do you focus on price and other feature comparisons? Are you satisfied with the percentage of your qualified prospects who decide to buy?

Consider: *Do you feel in control as you* ***buy****? Do you have choices for how you can complete a purchase? Does the company use what it has already learned about you during the purchase or are you asked basic things again? You're out to breeze past this task and get on to solving your need. You hope to feel affirmed that you made a good decision.*

Assess: Does your purchase process contribute to or detract from a customer's sense of convenience and control? Do you **protect** your customers so they emerge from this process satisfied and affirmed (not captive and resigned)? Do you lose customers here?

From your *target customer's* point of view:

From your *organization's* point of view

Consider: *Are you able to* ***solve*** *your need? What first steps do you take to put this solution to work? If you need help, where do you turn? What happens to let you know the product or service is working? Did your earlier vision of life after your purchase come true?*

Assess: How well do your actions—and your product or service itself—**prove** the promise you made to solve your customer's need? How does your company know the problem was solved? Are you satisfied with your return on investment in service operations? Your operating margin?

Consider: *What do you think of the solution you bought and the company who sold it? Did it solve your need? Did you connect with them in a meaningful way? Do you hear from them again? (Do you want to?) Would you buy from this company again? How will your needs likely* ***evolve?*** *Will you experience the same need again, or perhaps something new? How, and to whom, will you communicate your thoughts?*

Assess: Do you follow up to see if your customer's need was solved? Do you **anticipate** their next need? Are you satisfied with your ability to retain and grow customer relationships? Do your customers advocate for or detract from your brand reputation when they share their point of view with others?

An incisive colleague of mine is fond of challenging his co-workers, friends and consultants with a powerful question after they give him a piece of information: "Do you know this, or do you *think* you know this?" I ask you to ponder the same question as you reflect on your reactions to the questions on the last few pages.

Where would you plot yourself on this spectrum of bases for understanding your answers?

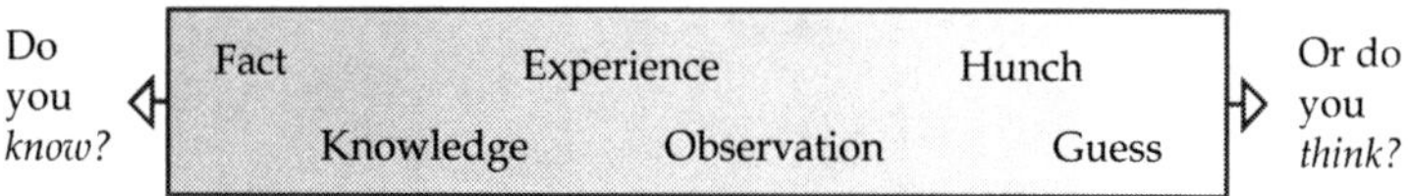

Don't lose heart if you're toward the "think" end of the spectrum. Your intuition, observations and even your own experiences as a customer all combine to give you a strong set of data from which to create a baseline assessment. Your employees throughout your organization also contribute to your available data across the spectrum. You don't have to be a strategic consultant to diagnose your organization. You just need to keep your eyes open. With just a few pages under your belt, you have enough to act.

You have defined "what is"

If only mentally, you have just created a basic map of your existing customer experience. You may also have an initial diagnosis of how effectively your customer experience is generating reward for your company.

It is possible that you are among the minority of leaders, that as you've read the last few pages and reflected on your organization's alignment, you realized that when asked "is your customer experience making you money," your answer is "Yes!" Even so, you may have spotted ways you can boost the financial and sustainability power of your customer experience. That will likely always be the case. Combine a recurring cycle with a need for alignment, and the result is typically an opportunity for ongoing refinement and recalibration.

But if you're like the majority of leaders...well, perhaps you're thinking that larger adjustments need to be made. If this quick diagnostic left you with the burning sensation that your customer experience costs your company lost revenues or leaks profits, you're not alone. And you face a wonderful opportunity.

Think about what could be

Say you had another map—one that shows what *ideally* would happen, and how your customers would *ideally* feel as they experience your solution.

To begin to see what that map looks like, imagine, from your customers' point of view, a need arising that your organization happens to be particularly well-suited to solve. Their problem is real and they will pay good money to solve it. Pay attention to what triggered that need. Picture your best prospect going to the first place that naturally came to mind to explore options for solving it, and picture that customer finding you conveniently on that path, as if there were nowhere else you could be.

Consider the words your customer uses to learn about you, and picture your response in that same vocabulary. Think of how your response might convey how your product or service could best help that customer solve his or her need, not how you might present a generic grid comparing the gamut of your offer's features and functionality to the competitors. Walk with your customer through a buying process in his or her location of choice, currency of choice, delivery method of choice and communication method of choice. Sit with that customer as he or she uses it, tries it and enjoys its solution. And watch as your customer begins to develop the next need, perhaps the same one again, or perhaps something different, something evolved. Repeat the cycle, picturing where your customer goes to start looking for options.

In the ideal scenario you just envisioned, your organization's actions are in perfect alignment with your target customer experience. You chose a target customer with a real problem worth solving. That means they'll value what you provide and never consider you a price-driven commodity. You maximize your revenue performance.

In this scenario you made great operating choices across your organization—product, service, marketing, operations, even people and investment choices—to solve your target customer's need better than anyone else. And since you're investing in what customers value and not in things they don't, you maximize profit.

This experience is an *ideal* view of how customers **realize** their need**, learn** about you, **try** you out, **buy, solve** their problem and **evolve** to their next need over time.

Inside your organization, this is an *ideal* view of how you **choose** a triggering need, **earn** consideration, **demonstrate** how you are different, **protect** customers as they buy, **prove** your promise and **anticipate** your customers' next need.

Using customer experience to drive real performance

You may feel this ideal view is just that—ideal. It may seem unachievable. That's okay. The real action (and your journey to reward) begins when you use this ideal customer experience as a *target.* It will provide purpose and context to every decision you make at your company. In other words, you can win a better performance payoff just by aiming at the target.

Here's how it can be done. Using customer experience to drive a performance reward requires two simple but big steps.

The first step is about setting direction—the "if" in an "if-then" statement, the customer experience to which you aim.

The second step is about execution—the "then," or the "what" that you must do.

The first requires you to understand your business from your customers' point of view. The second challenges you to align your actions with what your customers value to solve their problem.

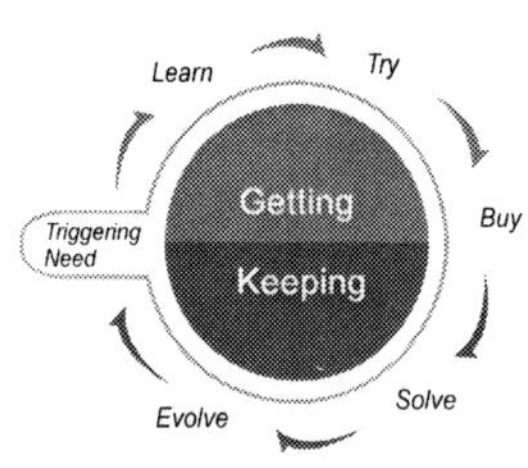

FIRST: Define a target customer experience map.

Show the most important things that *must happen* and *how customers should feel* at each step of the experience. Define this from your customer's point of view.

SECOND: Use your target customer experience for daily decision making.

Define the product, marketing, operations, organization structure, investment and service actions that align with your target experience. Define them from your organization's point of view.

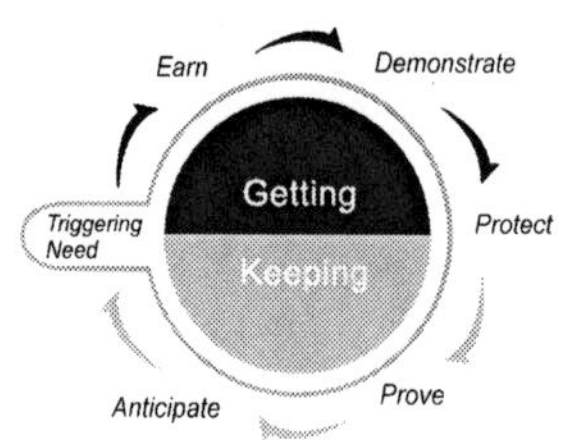

From service mantra to operating strategy

Does this sound like a radical change from what drives daily decisions in your organization today? When you use a target customer experience to drive daily decisions in your organization, you will certainly enjoy the improvements in customer service and loyalty you have come to expect.

You will also impact performance in your highest-level metrics—sustainable revenue and profit.

You won't make *new* decisions. You will still decide which customers are best to serve, which new ideas are worthy of investment, how you'll organize and execute. Yet by choosing the right problem to solve and bringing all of these actions into alignment with what solves it best and fastest, you will make all of those same decisions *differently*.

So now that you know this, I have a question for you:

Could you gain a valuable financial payoff if you used a clear target customer experience to drive all—or at least all of the most important—decisions your organization makes every day? I say yes.

> Use your target experience as an operating strategy that serves as the foundation for your day-to-day decisions and activities. Use it to create sustainable financial results.

What now?

If you considered the diagnostic questions on pages 12 - 14, you have a good running start on the journey you will take to find a performance reward in your customer experience:

1) You have a general understanding of your *existing* customer experience.
2) You have a basic *target* customer experience and a *target* organization experience.
3) You have a diagnostic point of view about the gap between how your organization is driving—or draining—performance reward.

4) You have a piqued curiosity about how to use a target customer experience in daily decision making to earn a better payoff.

Is your customer experience making you money? Enough? Costing you money? Too much? Now you have a pretty good idea.

Business leaders who understand the link between customer experience and financial performance are exceeding their performance targets, and they are sustaining that performance. They are translating their target customer experience requirements into actionable strategies and day-to-day decisions that generate real financial payoffs. For these leaders, there is no tradeoff between achieving ideal customer experiences and enjoying profits. They are using customer experience as the path to achieve sustainable financial performance.

Customer experience matters because it drives performance. My hope is that this book helps you execute on this simple and powerful idea, through daily decisions and actions. It is about how to get reward, and not punishment, from your customers.

Now *that's* a movement worth joining, yes?

How to use this book

Whether you solve one problem or many, whether you sell a single product or a global portfolio of products and services, I believe you will find a performance reward in the chapters that follow. Each chapter represents a step along the customer experience wheel, with actionable definitions to help you diagnose business performance implications for your company.

Next, you'll find questions, tools, exercises and metrics. These go deeper than the basic questions you answered in this chapter; they are designed to help you create a usable map for each step of your target customer experience. Some require you to see things from your customers' point of view. Others help you align your company's daily actions with your customers' target experience.

You'll see not only what to do, but also, through a list of key operating metrics, what to measure as you use your target experience to make the daily decisions that can reap your first or largest reward.

I have included an example or two in each chapter to bring the concepts to life. Most of them are culled not from our client base, but from my own personal observations, to underscore the point that you, too, can see this book's principles in action by keeping your eyes open as a customer everywhere you go.

You can read chronologically, taking in the entire set of customer experience steps before you begin. Or, you can get grounded in chapter 2 and then work the remaining steps in order of importance to your organization.

Do you have an instinct or indication that you can make the biggest performance change by focusing most on one specific step? If so, you might go straight to the exercises and tools in that chapter.

Less sure where to start? Skim the definition, text and diagnostic questions that open each chapter, and use your initial evaluation to decide where to go from there.

On pages 216 - 217, you will find a full experience map with room to collect ideas as you work through the book.

Chapter 2: First *Why*, then *What*

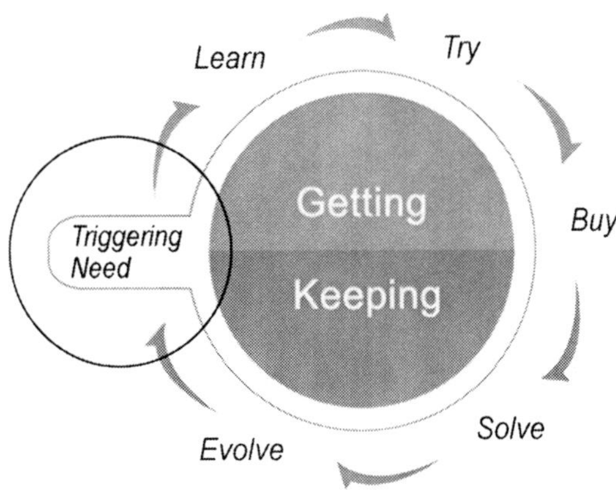

What you solve is more important than what you sell.

In the real beginning, there are no products or services. There are only needs or desires. Long before a prospective customer reaches out to engage you, he or she has a need.

Mom wants family memories; she considers her options and then decides on a digital camera. A corporate executive wants her brand name to roll off the tongues of teenagers, so she tries credible ideas and then selects an advertising agency. A hospital that wants to become a magnet for a patient care specialty buys the most advanced new piece of surgical equipment. A teenager is thirsty; he instinctively grabs a bottle of juice.

In each case, the basic need—you might even call it an instinctive or primal need—is rarely stored side by side with any specific product or service in your prospect's thoughts. For your target customer, the triggering need is defined as:

TRIGGERING NEED:
The essential problem or desire that motivates your target customer to look for a solution.

At this step, your target customer simply realizes a need. Needs can be proactive (a traveler needs to know how she will get around Argentina during her family's upcoming vacation). They can also be reactive (a hurricane causes water damage to the floors in an office building and the property manager needs it fixed quickly).

From your company's perspective, the triggering need is the choice of what problem, for which target customer, your organization will solve. It sets the focus for everything you do (and correspondingly, the lack of focus for companies who fail to clearly define it).

The problem you solve is the headwaters of the river of demand for your company. It should be the *why* your organization does *what* it does.

For your organization, the triggering need is defined as:

TRIGGERING NEED:
The essential problem or desire your company seeks to solve for a defined target customer.

Everything starts here. Why? Because customers don't buy products or services. They buy the absence of pain or the fulfillment of a desire. For this reason, solving a problem will generate a more sustainable performance reward than selling anything.

For you, the triggering need is all about defining the purpose that sets you on a path to achieve the revenue and profit reward you seek. You will continue to measure outcomes in products, services and associated dollars, yet you will define your target market and focus your actions by problems solved for a defined market segment.

To *drive* performance reward, what you solve is more important than what you sell.

Start here, always. This remains true whether you're working with a prospect or an existing customer. It holds true for your current value proposition and for the ones that will evolve over time.

Because everything you do—your entire operating strategy—flows from the triggering need, I can't overstate the importance of getting this step right.

To get the most performance reward, I'm suggesting you do two things here. First, identify what problem you are offering to solve, restating your purpose to align with your customer's triggering need. And second, evaluate whether the problem you are addressing suits your *target* customer, and that you are uniquely well equipped to solve it.

Right problem, right customer?

If you align all of your operating actions with solving a problem well for the right target customer, you will make more money. Test your problem against the following three criteria. If you can agree that all of these statements are true for your organization, then you will succeed.

- *There are enough customers who have the problem.* "Enough" is a big enough group of like-minded customers in which your company will invest. This creates sufficient market size.
- *The need is real.* "Real" means the problem is important enough to those who have it that they will pay meaningful money to make it go away. This creates the opportunity for top-line revenue, as well as a meaningful profit margin, because customers don't commoditize or push prices down for real solutions to important problems.
- *You can solve the problem well.* This sets you up for successful execution and renewable growth. "Well"

means solving the problem better than the alternatives available.

I will state it again, and not for the last time in this book: the key is alignment of your operating actions—your company's experience if you will—with your target customers' experience at every step. The challenge of this chapter is to be sure that you have chosen to solve the right problem for the right customer.

The problem you solve should be the underlying reason for the decisions you make every day in your organization. Is it? This seemingly simple question is often devilishly difficult to answer.

The problem you solve is also the test your customers use to decide if doing business with you is a good idea. From the moment they meet you, they judge everything you do by whether they believe you can solve their problem, whether they feel you did solve their problem and, if so, how well.

Choose the problem to solve wisely.

Connecting who to what

There are a lot of moving parts to think about as you make this choice. First and foremost is an accurate description of your ideal customer, and nailing that isn't easy. It is tempting to be liberal in defining them. *"Anyone in the world should want what I have to offer! More is better, right?"* Not necessarily. If you consider almost everyone a target customer, then those who can drive growth and profitability for you will find it difficult to identify with you.

They won't see themselves as any different from those who have only *some* of the characteristics that underscore a rewarding relationship. As a result, they will pass you by, and that's a revenue drain. Even worse, attracting customers who are a less than perfect fit for the problem you can solve well will be a distraction for your sustainable performance. They will "gunk" up your business processes, service levels and decision making as you try to make the problem you really do solve fit theirs (which you really don't solve well). And, you guessed it—that's a profit drain.

Defining your target customers correctly means knowing about them. Yes, you should do research, but it does not have to be costly or complicated. In fact, if you think the only research worth doing is the kind you can call "statistically significant," you may want to suspend your version of reality for a moment.

Select a group of customers who are representative of your business today. You'll likely need fewer than 30, because clear themes will emerge after as few as 10 conversations. Ask them why they use your product or service and what problems it solves for them. You are going after why they choose you over the competition, sure, but the heart of what you need to know is *what the product or service they buy from you solves for them*. Why is their life better because you are in it?

Just how big is your "who?"

Wise business leaders proactively measure the depth and breadth of the market they work to serve. As I mentioned in the criteria for success a few pages ago, your target customers should be a large enough group to provide a substantial and sustainable target market. Your target market is the sum of your best prospects.

You can define these as equations:

For existing problems:

Multiply the number of customers (current and potential) who have this problem by the dollar amount they each currently spend. The result is the size of your target market.

Number of customers with the problem we can solve

X the $ they spend to solve this need

= $ value of your target market

For newly identified problems where you are educating the market:

Multiply the number of customers with this problem by how much they would spend to solve it (think about how much it could be worth to them in dollars to make the problem go away). The result is the size of your new, potential target market.

Number of customers with the problem we can solve

X the $ it's worth to them to solve this need

= $ value of your potential target market

The promise of the triggering need

You can exercise control over the size of your target market, once you have precisely defined the problem you solve and the customers for whom you solve it. You have defined the fundamental need or want that sends your best prospects on their way to you. And you know it is a need that you can solve and solve well.

Do you know what *triggers* their need? This question is puzzling for leaders who are mentally locked into *selling* products and services rather than *solving* needs. If you are selling, you do not care what triggers a target customer's need because your acquisition and retention programs are geared to "push" — an operating strategy once described as "spray and pray." In contrast, a focus on what triggers a target customer to act will pay off richly in financial reward, because customers with needs are your promise of demand.

What can you do to increase the number of prospects who realize that same need or problem? Or the frequency with which your current customers have that need or want? Be there when the realization occurs. Increase the occurrence of the event if you can.

Let's say you sell insulated home siding. You may not *really* want to experience the coldest winter in 100 years in order to see increased demand for your product. (I live in Minnesota. The thought alone is cruel.) But if you're thinking that what you sell is a way to reduce the energy cost of homeownership in winter, sinking temperatures might come as great news to you. You're not selling siding; you're solving a problem. A cold winter is a triggering need you can translate into a peak in demand.

Work in this chapter if you don't have or don't like your answers to these questions:

Are you satisfied with the size of your target market?

Do you know which of your current customers drive the lion's share of your growth and profits? (Watch out: this may be two separate questions: Which customers drive your growth and which drive your profits? They may be vastly different sets.)

Are you satisfied with your ability to identify the best prospective customers for your organization?

Does your organization proactively generate demand? (For example, if you run the pharmacy inside a hospital, do you proactively create ongoing demand from people who live in the surrounding community, or do you assume you are there solely to fulfill prescriptions for patients?)

What problem or need do you have a reputation for solving well?

Is everyone in your organization focused on the problem you solve, or on something else?

To (re)define the triggering need your organization should endeavor to solve, let's take a look at the goals and actions of this step from your customers' and from your company's points of view:

Your customer's experience

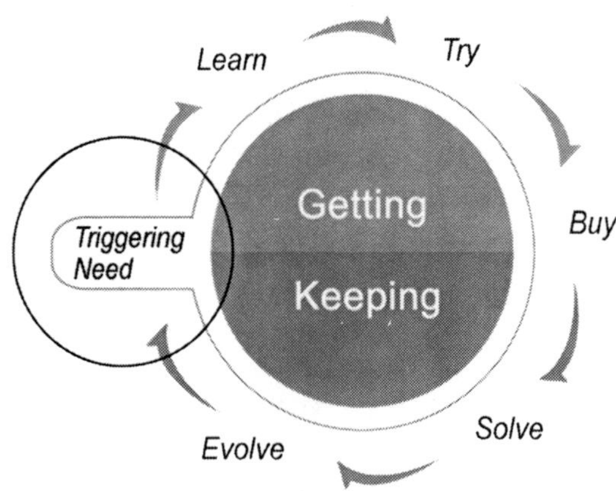

Their goal: Realize they have a real problem worth solving.

Their actions:

- Respond to a triggering event.
- Realize a need.
- Decide the need is real.
- Evaluate whether the need is important enough to merit solving.
- Define "solving it." Consciously or subconsciously, decide how life would be different and better if this problem or need were solved.

Your organization's experience

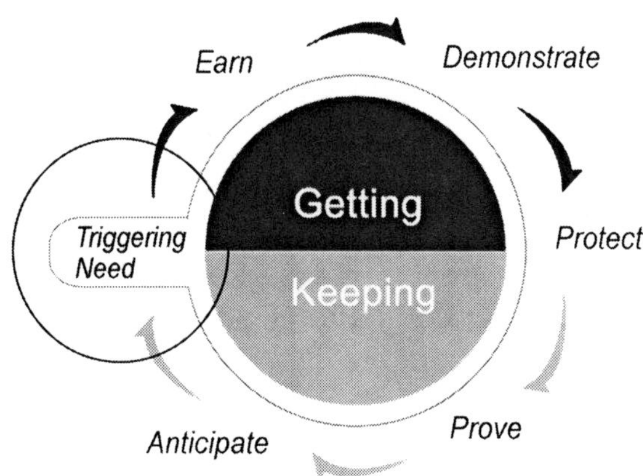

Your goal: Choose a problem to solve that generates demand.

Your actions:

- Define your target market.
- Determine and define what problem you can solve well.
- Find events that trigger a need.
- Where possible, increase events that trigger a need.
- Measure your effectiveness: you need a clear problem for a defined market segment large enough to fuel sustainable growth.

Use the work of others to spark your actions

Here are a couple of examples that are particularly illustrative of the work you need to do:

Northwest Architectural Salvage: How new problems can be good for business

For decades, this modest shop in Minneapolis' historic warehouse district has served as a unique source for restored antique home hardware—doors, stained glass windows and window panes, claw foot tubs and plumbing fixtures, fireplace mantels, doorknobs, hinges and more. The need that it solves, arguably, is *creating a sense of time, place and antiquity* in a home. The target customer was the homeowner who values history and antiquity in home architecture and design.

By 2007, however, I noticed the company capitalizing on a new target customer group and an additional need it could solve well: People who valued re-use of existing materials in their home as a means of reducing waste and energy. The need to be solved for this customer base was a bit different. These customers were out to *fulfill a sense of responsibility and awareness*—perhaps in addition to a sense of antiquity—in a home.

Having realized this emerging need, Northwest Architectural Salvage had identified a new problem to solve for a new target market. In later customer experience steps, the company would capitalize on existing products and adjust operating decisions like sales channels and staff knowledge to meet the new triggering need.

One company. One product line. Yet the identification of two target customer groups and two triggering needs to solve leads to a bigger pipeline of demand and room to grow.

Xcel Energy: The right problem for the right people

Getting a handle on a piece of new technology is hard enough on a personal basis. Imagine trying to implement technology change successfully for more than 12,000 employees. Not easy work.

Facing several enterprise-wide technology changes, leaders at Xcel Energy, a multi-billion-dollar energy company, wondered whether a customer experience-driven approach would earn them more employee satisfaction and less work disruption.

(Note: In this case, the "customers" having the experience were Xcel's employees.)

Many business and technology leaders might unfortunately define the problem to be solved in this kind of situation as follows:

> **Employee-customers** want to be happy with technology change. This is sometimes unrealistic, because some enterprise changes—like security upgrades—are mandated, not optional for employees.
>
> **Business and technology leaders** want enterprise-wide projects to be delivered on time and under budget. This can require a trade-off, as employees' needs and preferences appear last on the priority list.

Xcel leaders were thinking differently. They wisely spotted the opportunity to reframe the problem to be solved as one that could promote mutual self interest for employees and the business. The mutual need to be solved: plan, design, implement and digest technology change to maximize organization performance.

> **For employees,** maximizing organization performance means minimal disruption to their

functional work—be it in field operations, sales, finance or customer care.

For business and technology leaders, maximizing performance means planning the scope, sequence, training and communication of projects to flow as naturally as possible into functional work.

Approaching this problem through a comprehensive customer experience view, Xcel gathered a cross-functional team of technical, communications and project managers. This group participated in ideation and mapping sessions to determine the global impact that the suite of proposed changes would have on individual employees and their work, as well as on the organization overall. They created a target "employee-customer" experience map based on this target employee's needs during the change process. The map was then translated into a broader customer experience model of the technical actions and formal roles needed for successful technology change in the future.

Leaders at Xcel are on their way to positive outcomes that will have a big impact on how technology change is coordinated and communicated now and in the future. This is an example of how clearly defining the problem to be solved can result in measurable performance reward down the line.

The *Customer* Point of View

(Mapping your target customer experience)

Exercise 2.1
Who am I, anyway?

This step of the experience is about matching a problem you can solve well to target customers who will pay to make that problem go away. Let's start with defining who they are, and what triggers their journey to you.

One of your most valuable customers just took a seat in the chair right next to you. Imagine him saying who he is, how he behaves and what influences him.* Then, describe a need or problem he is willing to pay substantial money to eliminate.

My Demographic Profile (tangible descriptors)	*My Behavioral Profile (intangible motivators)*
Gender:	Price:
My job:	Cost:
Where I work:	Quality:
My title:	Reputation:

My Demographic Profile (tangible descriptors)	*My Behavioral Profile (intangible motivators)*
My family:	Convenience:
Where I live:	Control:
My age:	Knows you because:
My income:	Peer use / opinions:
My budget :	Protecting / serving:

** These are basic demographic and behavioral customer characteristics. Use what you know about your target customers to edit or adapt them. If you are still unsure, use the research and observation exercises that follow to define characteristics that best fit your situation.*

Keep thinking from your customers' point of view, and answer:

What words do I use when I think about or articulate my need, desire or problem to a friend?

Did something happen to make me realize my need?

Exercise 2.2
Define the problem or need you solve

Quick! Name the problem you solve for your best customers. You may NOT use the functional or proper name of your product or service in your answer:

Exercise 2.3
Let your customers tell you what you solve

In my work with clients who are struggling to understand what problem they best solve for their target customers, I often prescribe an informal series of brief interviews with their profitable, ideal customers. Usually fewer than 30 of these one-on-one conversations are required before patterns and clarity emerge.

Use the following as a template for the questions you ask. You may want to focus on a single product or service from your line, or steer the conversation to a higher level about your value proposition overall.

Question to ask existing customers	Payoff for knowing this
How important is my product or service to you? Why?	Gut level assessment of the degree of need
What does my product or service do for you? What does it enable you to do, to have or to be?	Inkling of problem solved
What would you do if you no longer had this product or could no longer use this service? What if the thing or the act went away as an option for you?	Why life is different because your solution is in it
What would be the impact on you?	The role your solution plays for them—the *tangible* effects it has
How would you feel?	More on the role your solution plays—the *intangible* effects
What might you substitute for my product or service? What if that substitute were no longer available? What would you try next?	A snapshot of your true competitors, including, perhaps, those who solve the same problem as you from a radically different approach

Exercise 2.4
Let them *show* you what problem you solve

Asking customers to tell you what problem you solve may not always work. Perhaps you don't have the money, time or access to ask them. Customers often have trouble articulating their needs. Sometimes they simply don't want to think about it.

Spend a day witnessing your target customers at any step of the customer experience—although to see the problem you solve, observe them where and when they are most likely to realize they have a need.

Shadow them on their job, listen as they talk to their friends and coworkers, watch what they say, do and feel as they realize they have the need and begin to try to address it.

If you sell prom dresses, hang out at the fashion magazine rack or at the department store and observe. If you sell legal information to the corporate librarians of large global law firms, ask a loyal client to let you shadow her on the job for a day during budget planning.

Your goal is to collect insight on the topics listed in the table on the next page:

What to watch for as you observe customers where they work / live / buy	Payoff for understanding this
What are they doing directly before they use your product or service (or an alternative)?	An inkling of the triggering event that causes them to realize a need or desire
What does the product or service do for that customer?	A concept of the problem you solve
What alternatives do they talk about, reach for, use?	A definition of the need from their point of view—shows you the common solution *they* see among alternatives
What words do they use? Do they talk with friends or peers?	More definition of the need or desire from their point of view, and insight into how they feel

Key performance indicators for the TRIGGERING NEED step

Is your customer experience making you money or costing you money? Here's how to arrive at the answer. Your actions' impact on business in this step is measurable in the following operating metrics. If you are not monitoring these items already, you may want to start doing so, or at least take a one-time baseline measurement to help you assess your success down the line.

I have noted which metrics are leading indicators (those that are predictive of future results) and which are lagging (those that reactively measure reward outcomes).

Leading → Size of your current target market—a signal that the target customer and problem you have chosen to solve are clear and able to drive sustainable demand

Leading → Growth rate of your target market—driver of your growth potential

Leading → Size of current target customer pipeline, in customers and dollars, to measure your effectiveness in generating demand from the target market

Lagging ← Overall revenue and profit per customer—an indicator you've chosen the right target customer, and are solving a problem effectively

Lagging ← Overall product profitability—more indication that your customer and organization actions are in alignment and delivering reward

If you were playing *Monopoly®*, the triggering need would be your GO spot. The game starts here, and as you go around the board you'll return here cyclically, and often. If you cannot get to a clear definition of the need you solve, stop here. Do not pass GO, do not collect your $200. And definitely, absolutely do not invest your time and precious money in product design, pricing decisions, process improvement or fast supply chains.

Remember the old proverb, "If you don't know where you're going, how will you know if you get there?" Making any decision without knowing what clear customer need to solve is at best a waste of time. More realistically, it's a big waste of your profits. Consider yourself well-aligned to your target customer experience at this step when the problem you solve well is directed at a substantial market segment of customers who will pay money to solve it.

Move to the next chapter if you can confidently say these things about…

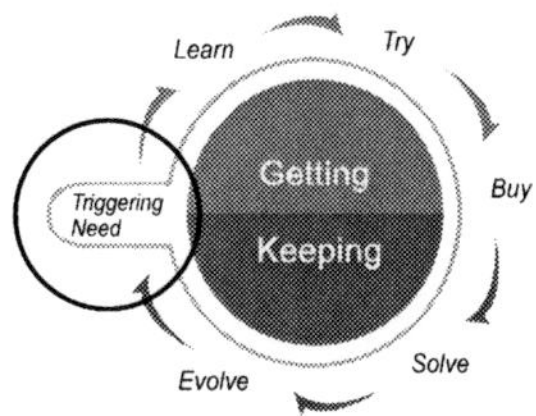

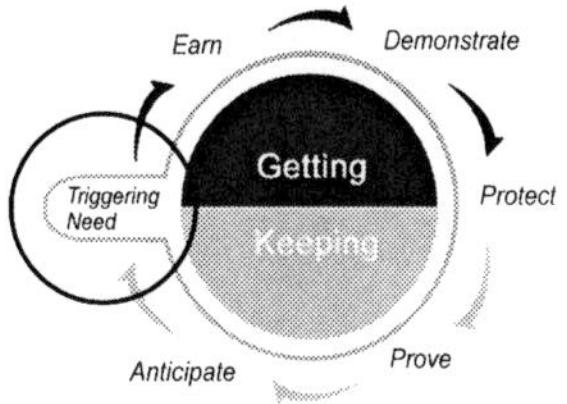

…your customer's target experience:

I know what triggers my customers to realize that they have a need, problem or desire.

I know the language target customers use to describe their need or problem to a friend or peer.

I know what target customers are feeling when they realize their need.

When my target customers picture the need solved, it looks like this:

____

…your organization's target experience:

We know the demographic and behavioral profile of our target customers.

We know the real problem we solve well.

Our target market is _________ big, and we have sufficient room for growth.

We know our customers' triggering events.

We proactively increase triggering events.

We lead the _________ position in the market place.

Chapter 3: Get in the Way (In a Nice Way)

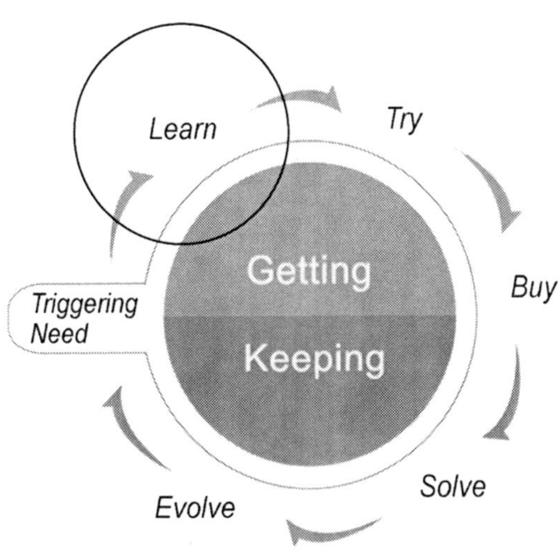

You can't convert demand you don't have, and you can't convert the wrong demand effectively.

Now it begins. Your customer has a problem or need, and either proactively or reactively, instinctively or with great deliberation, he or she will begin the search to solve it. At this step, your customer is out to create a short list of good options. This may occur in a brief instant—"I'm thirsty. Where is the nearest soda machine?"—or as a reaction triggered by an event such as seeing a billboard, hearing an idea from a peer or experiencing a car accident. Often it happens over time through initial exploration and observation of others. Your prospect is simply narrowing down all of the possibilities to the few options worthy of deeper consideration. For them, learn means:

LEARN:
To search for and collect options that appear credible to solve a problem.

The LEARN step starts the instant after your prospect realizes they have a need. It ends when he or she has created a short list of good options.

What makes an option worthy? What does "good" mean? Good options generate a simple statement of confidence in your prospect's mind: "That looks like it might work for me." This might come across as a low standard. It is not low. It's *personal.*

- "Good" in your prospect's eyes defines something that looks like a credible idea to solve their problem.
- Good options may span a broad spectrum of approaches to solving the problem. If my problem is a stiffness in my neck, I may choose a different pillow, a yoga class, a massage or a pain reliever. If my problem is cutting the waste out of my company's supply chain, I may consider an internal team, a consultant or new suppliers.

This is mental triage. It is carried out by instinct, based on the knowledge and perceptions your prospect already has. He is thinking "maybe this one; certainly not that one; my sister told me that one is great..."

Prospective customers need this discreet step before trying things in more detail, and whether they are conscientiously are aware of it, they will go through it every time. When shopping for cars we select a small number to test drive, based on appearance, price and perceived performance. When a benefits administrator shops health plans for the company's employees, he or she chooses candidates based on reputation, breadth of coverage, quality, price, relationship and any number of other qualities.

From your company's perspective, your goal at this step is simply to make the target customer's short list of good options. Said differently, you must *earn* their consideration.

EARN:
To plan and take the deliberate steps that win a prospect's consideration and a place on their list of credible options.

There are three requirements for your organization to achieve the payoff of consideration (translation: a hefty pipeline of demand):

1) *Be in the right place at the right time.* Help your customers find you easily, when and where they naturally go looking. Even better, discover what your customers are doing when they first realize they have a need, and be there.

2) *Talk to your customers in their language.* Use their vocabulary, and encourage everyone in your organization to understand and relate to their state of mind and attitudes at this step. This means translating everything - from your business cards to your web site page titles to your personal answer to the question "what does your company do?" – from business-speak to the words customers use to describe their need and solution to a peer.

3) *Know when to stop talking.* Have the discipline, patience and confidence to do and say just enough to introduce yourself. Your goal here is to make the short list, not secure the win. The marketer in all of us wants to share everything we want a customer to know. Resist.

Reflect on the criteria your customer will use to draft the short list. Since their goal here is to find merely reasonable options and *not* the perfect answer (yet), they may consider a more broad set of ideas than you may expect. In fact that may or may not even include you and your direct competitors or substitutes.

Customers will consider both tangible qualities (the cost and size of that Hummer 3 compared to a compact car) and intangible ones (emotional thoughts like "I would never drive a Hummer" or "That Hummer will make me the envy of my block.")

Why is it important to get this step right? Where does it fit into earning payoff from your customer experience? Simple: You can't convert demand you don't have, and attracting the wrong demand leads to a drain of profits and a loss of a "right revenue" opportunity.

Debate theorists say one of the best ways to get someone enthusiastic about your idea is to make him think he came up with it on his own. As you approach the step of earning your way onto your customers' short list, that's a powerful bit of wisdom. Literally or figuratively, conscientiously or without a deliberate thought, your target customer walks a path that begins at having a need and ends at a list of viable solutions to solve it.

You want to be on that path in clear sight, your promising solution shining like a beacon. It should seem as though you belonged squarely on that path, as though there were nowhere else you would rather be. Your customer will be proud for having thought of you.

You want target customers, not any customers

Remember that you are trying to do this for the right customers. The richest reward comes from those prospects who have the need you solve and who fit the demographic and behavioral profiles of your most profitable customers.

Trying to be everything to everyone will cost you more money than you'll earn. Trying to be the right thing for the right people will yield the largest financial payoff.

Get this step right, and your pipeline of demand will flow with the right kind of customers who investigate you because you are a credible option to solve the need you want to solve. You will boast a healthy return on your marketing and lead generation expenses. Later on, customers will say that your company or product brand matches your rightful position in the marketplace - solving the problem you want to solve for the customers you want to serve.

This won't happen because you are a good person, or because your logo is attractive, or even just because your product is the best in the world. It will happen because you earned it.

Work in this chapter if you don't have or don't like your answers to these questions:

Are you satisfied with the size of your demand pipeline? Do you have *enough* prospects?

Are you attracting the *right kind* of prospects? Or do you find yourself welcoming prospects that in the end aren't profitable or loyal?

Are your target customers aware of your brand?

Are they naturally where you look for them? Are you where they naturally look for options?

What are the two most important criteria your target customers use to narrow down their options to a short list?

What alternatives do your target customers use instead of your products or services to solve their need or problem? Do you define competitors by what you sell or by the problem you solve? (The latter is better.)

Are you getting a good return on your investment of money and time in finding target customers?

To (re)define your thoughts on how you can best earn your way onto your target customers' short list, let's take a look at the goals and actions of this step from your customers' and from your company's points of view:

Your customer's experience

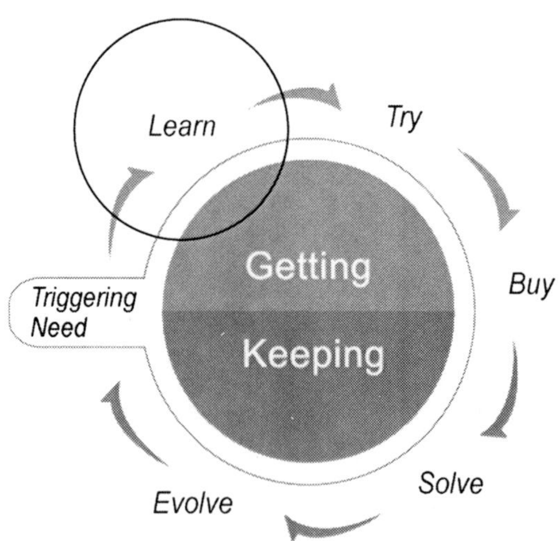

Their goal: Make a short list of good options to consider further.

Their actions:

- Act on instinct.
- Scan viable solutions and substitutes.
- Know what "good" means (criteria for making the list).
- Narrow down solutions to a few, and create a "short list" for further consideration.

Your organization's experience

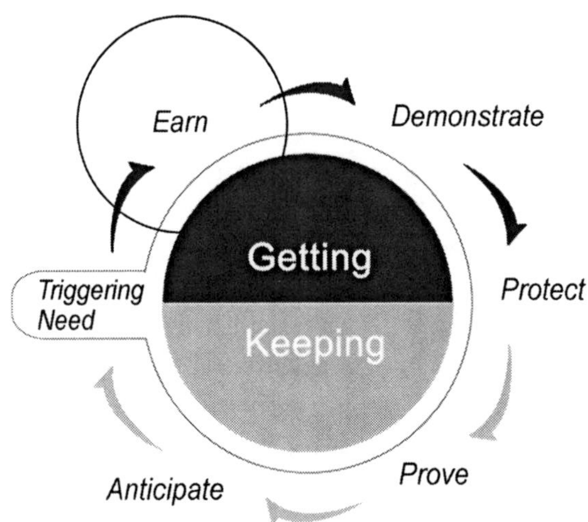

Your goal: Earn consideration and make the short list.

Your actions:

- Find out where prospects realize they have a need.
- Place yourself in the path of your learning customer.
- Get noticed.
- Learn what criteria they use to narrow their options.
- Make it fast—convey the problem you solve and why you're unique in the moment prospects scan options.
- Define the problem and your solution in your customer's language.
- Say and do just enough to earn consideration.
- Measure the size of your demand pipeline and the percentage of attainable customers who choose you for their short list.

Use the work of others to spark your actions

Here is an example that illustrates the work you may need to do:

Paint Shop Pro Software: five seconds to make the list

If you're selling a photo-editing software from Jasc Software (recently acquired by Corel Corporation of Canada), earning the consideration of new digital camera owners requires standing out against, or at least achieving par with, two little competitors called Microsoft and Adobe. Without the millions those market leaders can afford to spend to ensure they get premium positioning in retail stores, Jasc found itself on very crowded shelves.

Packaging is the attention-getting device of choice in retail. Some experts declare that prospects spend no more than five seconds glancing at options before deciding which, if any, boxes to pick up and study in more detail. Jasc's packaging focused on price, rebates or freebies to get the attention of prospective buyers. Faced with being perceived as a #3 player competing on price, Jasc decided to redouble its focus on the problem it knew it could solve well for target customers, and reshape its packaging to match.

Through the company's customer research and open feedback channels, Jasc's digital camera customers confided that they enjoyed taking pictures and they enjoyed sharing pictures. Everything in between… not so much. Many felt that what came after the snap of the shutter and before the photos were ready to share was the part of owning a digital camera that interested them least. Jasc saw in this new information a problem it could solve well.

To get from shutter snap to sharing photos happily, camera owners were clear about their first and most important needs: Crop photos. Fix red eye. And organize photos so they can be found and shared easily. The research drove the package redesign.

Before:	Emphasis on price and $100 of free software filters included in the box
After:	Declaration that Jasc is the award-winning software for cropping photos, fixing red eye and organizing photos

It worked. Sales in these retail stores increased 20 percent, and Jasc protected product margins.

Exercise 3.1
Discover your real competition

Quick! Name at least three alternatives your target customers use *instead* of your product or service to solve their need. Hint: The landscape of good options is always broader than the list of your direct competitors.

1.
2.
3.
4.
5.

Exercise 3.2
Scan the full landscape

Imagine you are one of your target customers, and you've just realized you have the need, problem or desire that your firm can solve well.

See the *full* landscape from your prospect's perspective. What options are visible? What options appear along the road you normally travel?

Alternatives I may find (or that may find me)	Product Options	Service Options	Do it Myself Options	Do Nothing Options

Exercise 3.3
The first thing I do is…?

Imagine you are one of your target customers, and you've just realized you have the need, problem or desire that your firm can solve well.

What is your natural first course of action? In other words, what do you instinctively do first? List as many possible first steps you can think of.

Proactive or reactive steps I take to create my short list of good options	Talk to a friend or colleague	Go online and search the problem	Reconnect with options I already know	Collect options that cross my path

Once you have a comprehensive list of possible first steps, circle the top two or three your *target* customers are most likely to do first.

BONUS Exercise 3.3
The first thing I do is...?

Are you thinking about doing research with customers, or perhaps already doing it? Here's an easy way to get more from that investment.

Add three simple sets of questions to your research:

What to ask customers	Payoff for knowing this
1. What does my product or service do for you? What does it enable you to do, to have or to be?	Validation of the problem solved—grounds everything you do
2. What's the first thing you do to find options that could solve your need?	Knowledge of where you must meet them in order to earn their consideration
3. What's the *next* thing you do to settle on the options you want to explore in detail? The next thing after that?	More knowledge—about where is the *next* most important place to meet them, and the next...

TIP: Use the list you created in the previous exercise ("The first thing I do") as your multiple choice options for questions 2 and 3.

Allow customers to mark what they do first, second, third. Leave room for "other" so you can learn what things you may be missing.

Your Organization's Point of View

(Defining daily actions that unlock reward)

Exercise 3.4
Shall we date?

Depending upon the problem your prospects have, learning about options and landing on a short list may take seconds or months. Regardless of the time they take, your prospects will judge you based on a basic, high level understanding of what you do and why you're different. They are looking for a great first impression. This is like speed dating; you don't have a lot of time.

To earn their consideration, define what *must* happen and how a prospect *must* feel to put you on their short list. There may be lots of possibilities, or even several process steps. That's okay.

Your goal here is to define the key success events—the things that must be there, or be there first. Building less important options and process steps around key success events will be easy later on.

What must happen or happen first of all?	*What must they feel, or feel first of all?*
___ An influencer must name us. Who:	___ Curious
___ They must see themselves in our visual presentation or brand style.	___ Excited

What must happen or happen first of all?

___ They must see the image of what they hope to be (an aspirational style)

___ They must see a price.

___ They must see someone else using our product or service.

___ Other:

What must they feel, or feel first of all?

___ Jealous (that someone else has what they need)

___ Calm

___ Relieved

___ Influenced

___ Invited

___ Other:

TIP: Use the list you created in "The first thing I do is…" exercise. Translate your customer's most likely actions into one or two *absolutely must-happen* events that you will create to earn consideration. Translate them again into the one or two things that your prospects absolutely must feel in order to put you on their short list of options.

Exercise 3.5
Location, location, location

Let's find out how easily your target customers are finding you, and how efficiently you're finding them.

In the table on the next page, list the locations where you spend most of your time and energy on marketing and/or advertising (i.e. "billboards along the Interstate," "our Web site," "responses to RFPs," "our annual trade show," "smooth jazz radio station ads," "public relations to build our reputation").

In the next column, consider the degree to which each place you currently focus is along the natural path of your *target* customer.

In the right column, note where your current focus matches where your *non*-target customers are found. Alignment here is *not* so good, and therefore you may see an opportunity to improve performance by redirecting your focus.

Location where we focus money and time to find target customers	Natural path of my target customers? (Circle one)	Natural path of *non*-target customers? (Circle one)
	No match Some match Perfect match	No match Some match Perfect match
	No match Some match Perfect match	No match Some match Perfect match
	No match Some match Perfect match	No match Some match Perfect match
	No match Some match Perfect match	No match Some match Perfect match

Exercise 3.6
It takes a village

If you have completed the exercises here and in the full experience map on pages 216 - 217, you probably have more than a few ideas about your target experience and how to use it. In most cases you may make many of the same decisions you always have, but now from a different, customer experience point of view. Some reward takes a village—a group of like-minded people who contribute different expertise, functions and accountabilities to the initiatives that re-set how things get done.

The purpose of the following two-part exercise is to define and prioritize the initiatives that require a village to get your reward. You will find this same exercise at the conclusion of most chapters, for use at each step along the customer experience wheel.

Part 1

Look back at your work in this chapter. What must you *stop, change or create* to move your organization into better alignment with your target customer experience?

- *Stop:* Things your company does that are in the way, or pulling you in a direction that doesn't match your target experience
- *Change:* Things you must keep doing, but do differently
- *Create:* Things that don't exist at your company or aren't done at all—but should exist or be done

List those things in the left column. Then, use your instinct and existing knowledge to say whether each initiative will take a small, moderate or huge amount of time, people and money.

Be inclusive! Think across disciplines to include finance, legal, IT, HR, sales, marketing, operations and the CEO.

Initiative to stop, change or create how things get done	People (Circle One)	Time (Circle One)	Money (Circle One)
❶	A FEW SOME A LOT	A LITTLE SOME A LOT	A LITTLE SOME A LOT
❷	A FEW SOME A LOT	A LITTLE SOME A LOT	A LITTLE SOME A LOT
❸	A FEW SOME A LOT	A LITTLE SOME A LOT	A LITTLE SOME A LOT
❹	A FEW SOME A LOT	A LITTLE SOME A LOT	A LITTLE SOME A LOT
❺	A FEW SOME A LOT	A LITTLE SOME A LOT	A LITTLE SOME A LOT

Part 2

Plot the actions you have listed on the previous page into the chart below, based on the estimates you made for time and effort ("doability" axis) and your estimate of the impact to financial performance reward each action will likely have ("impact" axis).

A reminder of the specific measures of performance for this step follows this exercise.

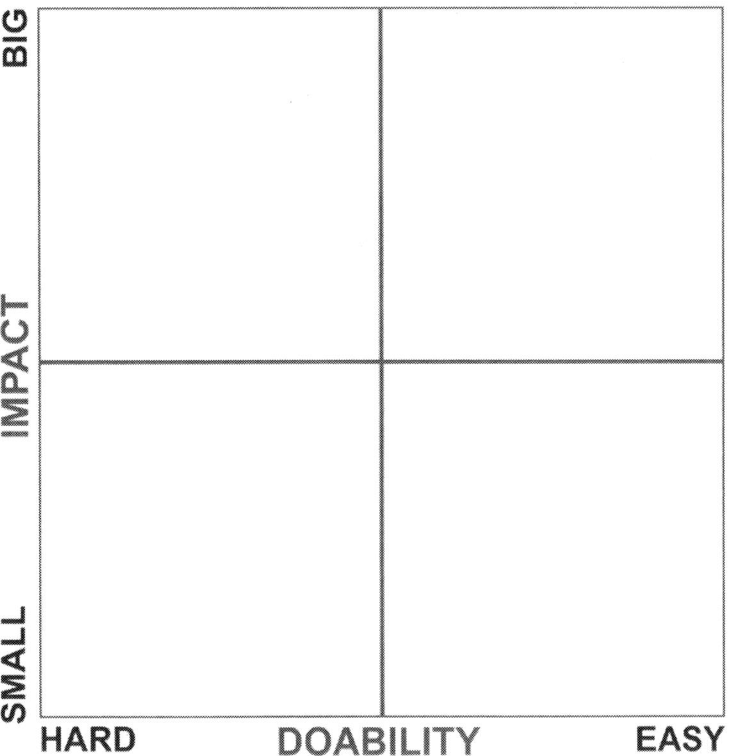

Once you have plotted your village initiatives, pick at least three (to gain traction) and no more than five (to keep things simple). Then go for it!

Key performance indicators for the EARN / LEARN step

Is your customer experience making you money or costing you money? Here is how to arrive at the answer. Your actions' impact on business in this step will be measurable in the following operating metrics.

If you are not monitoring these items already, you may want to start doing so, or at least take a one-time baseline measurement to help you assess your success down the line.

I have noted which metrics are leading performance indicators (those that are predictive of future performance) and which are lagging (those that reactively measure performance outcomes).

Leading → Number of prospects who consider your product, brand and company

Leading → Return on the sales/selling expenses you invest to earn consideration from your target customers

Leading → Return on investment of marketing expenses to generate leads or prospects, and to establish your product, service and company

Lagging ← Alignment between your brand's reputation and your desired position in the marketplace (i.e. for the problem you want to solve)

Making the short list might seem like a simplistic goal, but if you are weary from the battle to build a sufficient pipeline of the right kind of prospects, you know that "simple" is not necessarily easy.

The decisions you make and actions you take here determine how much of your target market is truly attainable for you. The more clearly and more quickly your target customers think "that looks like an option for me" the faster you will build your reward of a big pipeline of demand and effective return on your lead generation spending. You will also establish a barrier for the non-target customers who will punish you if they get into your pipeline.

Alignment here means you must earn consideration from (only) the target customers who have a problem you can solve well.

Move to the next chapter if you can make these declarations about…

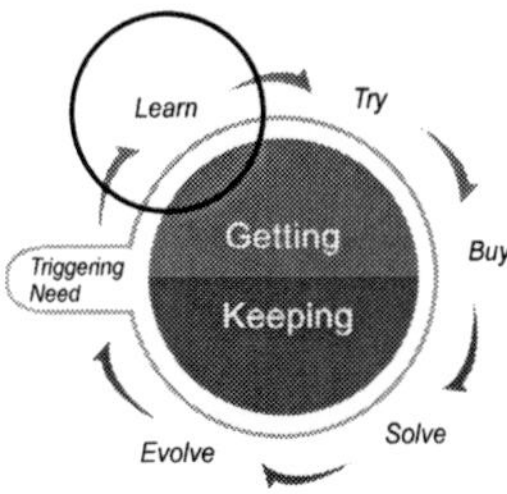

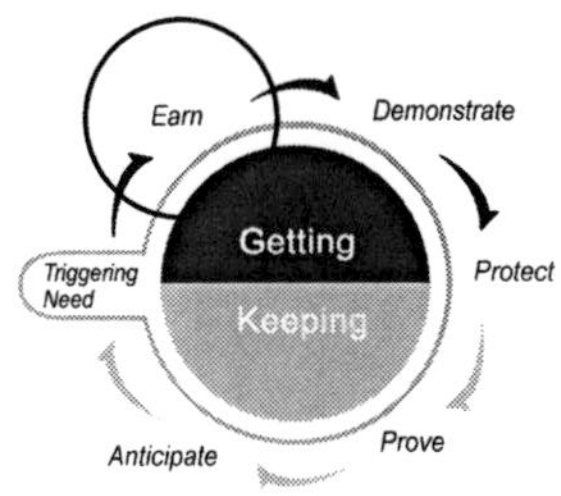

…your customer's target experience

We know what customers do first to learn about options.

We know the full range of options that will relieve their problem or need.

We know what words or ideas customers use to think about or search for options.

We know the tangibles and intangibles that must happen for our target customers to consider an option "good" or credible.

…your organization's target experience

We invest our time and money where our target customers look for options.

We see the full range of alternatives available to customers—and not just the obvious ones.

We use their language to open any interaction.

We design interactions so that events that earn a prospect's consideration always occur.

We are selected by our target customers. Non-target customers opt out.

Chapter 4: Virtual Reality

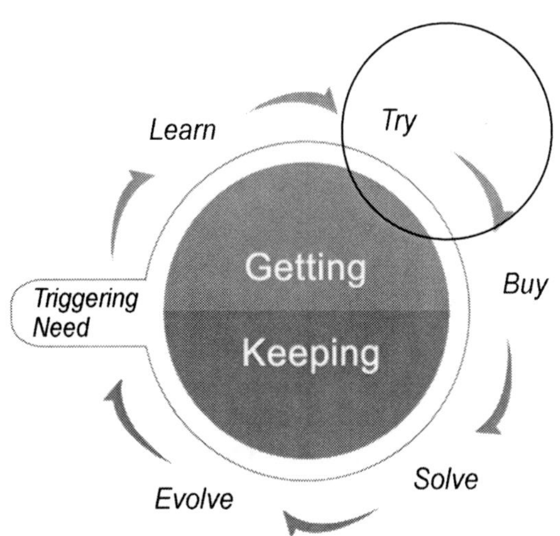

The more clearly prospects envision themselves with the problem solved, the more confidently they will choose how to solve it.

Once your target customer has realized a need and created a short list of good options, he or she will work to narrow the list to a single, best choice. During this step your prospect will imagine, evaluate, compare or literally try using your solution. The process may take only a moment when someone is selecting between two Pinot Noir wines to create a romantic dinner that night. When a small business is choosing an IT service firm to ensure business continuity for its customers, the TRY step may take months.

If you are like many of the leaders I meet, you are thinking this step is an interaction between you and your prospect. That is true, *and* it may also be an interaction between your prospect and a peer, colleague, friend or boss who will influence or approve the ultimate choice. Imagine the woman who takes two pairs of pants and three shirts into a dressing room and tries them on. She may be independent—mindful but not truly driven by what she imagines others may think of how she looks.

Often others play a direct role: a mid-level manager is the point person on the Request for Proposal process, yet he will facilitate evaluation and decision making with his boss and a cross-functional team of peers. Here, the prospect is definitely influenced by others, and perhaps even seeks approval from them.

TRY:

To build an understanding through experience and knowledge; to envision what life will be like after a potential solution to a problem has been applied.

This step begins when your target customer is ready to explore each option on the short list in more detail. It ends when she lands on a single option to which she is ready to commit (ideally yours).

For choices more complex than solving the "I'm thirsty" need, this step comes with some gnashing of teeth. To choose a final winner from a short list of all-credible options, your target customer must reject the other options, whether in one fell swoop or with the testing of one painstaking criteria after another. Psychologically, humans are not conditioned to let go of alternative courses of action without some amount of vulnerability. As a result, the intangible "chemistry" will certainly be on your prospect's criteria list, but he or she will also likely look for facts, feedback from trusted people and the opportunity to experiment, all in an effort to try out each option before making a confident choice to buy.

> Your prospects are out to envision themselves on the other side of the purchase, in the middle of a solved problem. You must build this virtual reality.

Sadly, some get stuck in this step, deciding that none of the options are right for them to solve their particular need. I say *stuck*—not finished—because their need or problem doesn't go away. Instead, they live with the problem and without a solution until some option demonstrates that it is best to help them solve it. In the worst cases, the TRY step takes years.

From your company's perspective, the goal is simple: target customers who confidently choose *you.* In other words, you must *demonstrate* why and how your organization or product or service is the best option to solve their need.

DEMONSTRATE:
To build an understanding through experience and knowledge; envision what life will be like after a potential solution to a problem has been applied.

If you do your job well here, your customers will do your qualification work for you, by falling out on their own if they are not your target prospects, and by feeling fully confident in choosing you if they are. The less you have to work to disqualify customers who are not your ideal, the less resources your sales efforts will require.

> You want your customers to choose the best option to solve their need. You want your target customers to choose you. You want the wrong customers to choose something else.

Most of us know when this is done well. Walt Disney World is an amusement park (what Disney sells) that uses planning CDs, podcasts and "create your own dream" tools that demonstrate how it helps *make family dreams come true* (the need or desire it solves). Target customers see themselves enjoying the trip before they have booked a ticket. Non-target customers, who may have only an afternoon to spare, who envision family togetherness in a more intimate setting or who do not have the budget, will likely self-select out of the experience. They save themselves money and time spent on the wrong family dream, and Disney saves the cost to serve an unhappy customer and avoids creating vocal detractors.

You may not have Disney's marketing budget, or a fun-to-visualize consumer need to solve, but the tasks and goals at this step are relevant for any organization.

Envision your target customers on the other side of the purchase with their problem solved well by you, and build that virtual reality. Design it so that the most important tangible things (like product and service features) and intangible things (like emotional cues or environment) are obvious and potent.

True at every step but particularly powerful here, the secret to revenue growth and sustainability is doing and asking your prospect for only those things that solve a need.

The requirements of virtual reality

Getting this step right (and achieving the rewards of a profitable close ratio and revenue growth) requires a few important things:

1) *Be problem-focused rather than competition-focused.* "Problem- focused" means that every benefit or feature you highlight demonstrates how you can solve the problem. You do not get drawn into feature-by-feature comparisons with competitors where unique, fast or big is the only goal. Why? Because the most unique or fastest or biggest feature in the world only matters if it solves a need that your target customer cares about and will pay you to solve.

2) *Understand the most important criteria a target customer will try out in order to make a choice.* "Criteria" means the tangible (such as process steps, price and product

or service benefits) and intangible (emotional) elements that are required in their virtual reality and inspire the customer to pick you.

3) *Design the experience so that the "virtual reality" of a problem solved unfolds in a natural sequence.* The information or actions you ask for should be designed so that target customers give or do what's most important to demonstrate the solution first, what's next most important happens second, and so on. This requires knowing the steps your target customers will most likely try first.

   It also means you use each of your channels of interaction (such as your Web site, sales people, print or other media) for what they do best. This is the reason complex product or service details are best presented online (rather than recited by a sales person), and rarely on the home page.

4) *You are attentive to a target customer's vulnerability.* "Vulnerability" is the natural hesitation or impulse to double-check that target customers have just before they make a choice. You must acknowledge it, using your product or service, process steps and information in a way that allows prospects to envision themselves on the other side of the purchase with a problem solved. Where influencers exist, enlist them in the virtual reality you create.

> The combination of tangible (price, features, process) and intangible (emotional cues) are part of a customer experience at every step. Here at the TRY step, though, they are particularly relevant. Your actions to demonstrate how you can solve a problem well can be highly potent.

Here are a couple of my favorite straightforward examples of how tangible and intangible elements can be designed together, demonstrating a solution and creating a "virtual reality" that moves prospects toward a confident choice. The first is real; the second is a goal of a leader I know.

In the lobby of my dry cleaner they have three shirts—one lightly starched, one medium, and one heavily starched—up on the wall like art at a museum. They have jeans too—not pressed, lightly pressed and pressed with crisp creases. Price and processing time appear next to each. Clothes just like mine. Freshly done. Tactile. When I want my professional clothes to make me look really professional, I know where to go.

Imagine a corporate travel company, hoping to win a three-year contract with a global prospect that needs better return on its travel investments during a time of rapid expansion. The travel company builds an "ROI calculator," where target customers can experiment with feature options and see their total investment per trip or per employee. They see the capacity in working hours created because employees are freed from long booking processes and taxi lines. After a nearly fun what-if experiment, the prospect can export a presentation for their boss for approval. A real bonus for both the travel company and the prospect: the session is used to pre-populate the formal sales proposal or presentation. The prospect sees the ROI and earns respect from her boss in the demonstration of it.

Same decisions you always *make, only different*

The emotions I'm talking about here are different from those that describe how your customers relate to the world around them, or to the emotional characteristics of your overarching company brand. Here your goal is to identify, understand and help target customers feel the emotions that *move them to you as the best choice to solve their problem.*

The number of *non*-target customers you welcome at this step has a huge impact on your customer retention rate and operating margins. If you let everyone in (after all, having more customers is always right, right?), you open yourself up after the sale to higher customer service and support costs. By trying to please non-target customers, you also nurture a larger audience of detractors who may speak out against your product, brand or company.

In this big step, think small: do (and ask for) only what is productive in getting your target customers further and fastest to a problem solved well.

Work in this chapter if you don't have or don't like your answers to these questions:

Are you creating an effective virtual reality for your target customers?

Can you name the most important tangible and emotional criteria that drive target customers to choose you?

Do you know who influences your target customers as they try options? Have you incorporated them into the experience?

How many of your *target* customers (the ones you would choose again) choose you to help them solve their need?

How many of your non-target customers (the ones you don't want) self-select out of your experience at this step?

Is your close ratio satisfactory?

Is your speed to close satisfactory?

Are you hearing "I didn't expect that!" in your service or feedback interactions after the sale?

To (re)define how you proceed from one choice on a short list to the ultimate chosen solution, consider the goals and actions of this step from your customers' and from your company's points of view:

Your customer's experience

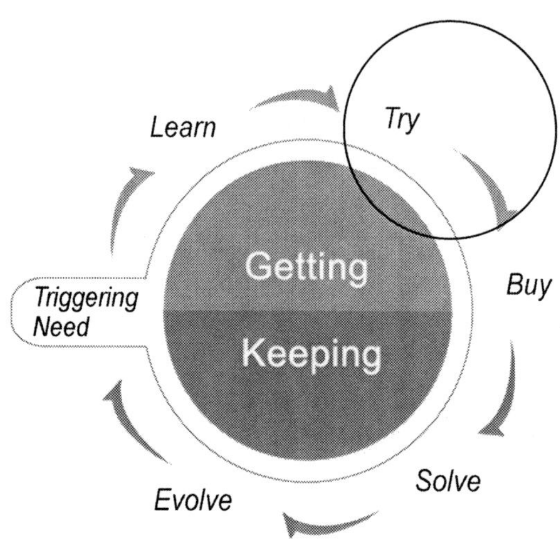

Their goal: Try out options to make a confident choice.

Their actions:

- Ask questions.
- Seek out evidence.
- Recall past experiences.
- Look for reinforcement or approval from those they trust.
- Experiment.
- Weigh priorities; decide what's important.
- Come to terms with a choice.
- Reject alternatives.

Your organization's experience

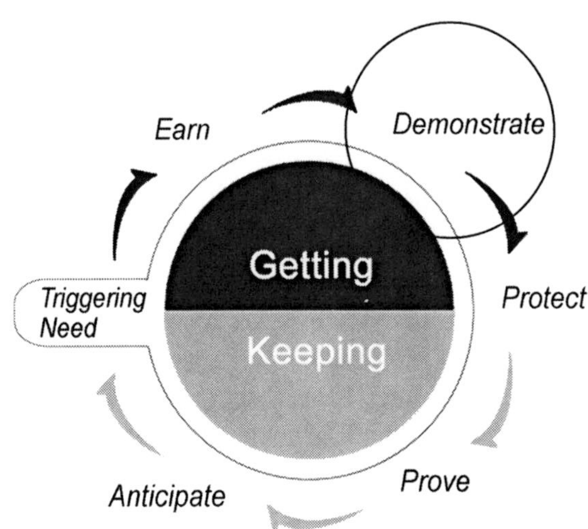

Your goal: Demonstrate why you're best to win their choice.

Your actions:

- Answer questions.
- Offer a taste, a sample, a view, a glimpse, a test.
- Build demos, simulations and experiments.
- Help them demonstrate your solution to their influencers.
- Be accessible in a way that's natural for them.
- Use sales channels and media for what they do best.
- Measure your return on acquisition efforts, and the ratio of target to non-target customers captured.

Use the work of others to spark your actions

These examples are particularly illustrative of the work you need to do:

Rush University Medical Center: The art of conversation

One in three Americans reports trouble sleeping at some point in their adult lives, as reported by the Rush Medical Center's Sleep Disorders Service and Research Center in Chicago. So imagine the calls that the center receives each day from concerned patients looking for treatment options—and consider how many of them are from people with short-term symptoms that merit nothing more than a referral to their general practitioner. I have noticed that organizations like Rush's Sleep Disorder Center that want to prevent routine information-gathering calls tend to do so by developing literature, especially brochures and Web sites, to replace work that would otherwise be done by more expensive salaried human beings. These solutions might work, but they don't reflect a caring alignment to the patient's experience, if what the patient wants to feel is protected and nurtured.

Enter the Rush Sleep Disorder Center's "Interactive Conversation," a 5- to 20-minute online experience that people with sleep problems can take on their own from any computer with a broadband connection. The tool asks, in a kind human voice backed up by identical words on screen, some simple questions, like whether the patient is troubled most by falling/staying asleep, nodding off during the day or snoring, and whether they've had the symptoms for a month or less, four months or less or more than four months. From there, Rush offers an initial recommendation (see a general practitioner first, give it another few weeks to see if your symptoms go away, have a brochure with sleep tips sent to you by email, make an appointment right away at the Sleep Disorder Center). It then asks the user to indicate whether she would like more information on her options, including Rush. The conversation is so well executed that the patient almost feels as if she is talking to a real human being. Thanks to several options to "move on or tell me more" throughout the conversation, Rush lets the patient control the pace and direction of the experience.

Rush is committed to both the art and the science of medicine, and its execution of the TRY step certainly fits the bill.

The interactive conversation, created by a company called Jellyvision, is available on the home page of the Rush University Medical Center Sleep Disorders Center (http://www.rush.edu/rumc/page-1099918808617.html).

Jellyvision also offers the conversation (and additional examples of such conversations it has created for other B2B and B2C clients), on its Web site at http://www.jellyvision.com.

Cisco Systems, Inc.: The virtual reality of virtual reality

At a time in history when the major news networks are experimenting with holograms on air and high-definition digital television is becoming the norm in every household, the business world is increasing its expectations for virtual communication solutions (virtual, as in "allow us to save travel money and be green but still feel like we're working together").

Cisco Systems, Inc., based in San Jose, California, is taking a big swing at solving that need. The company offers TelePresence, a face-to-face, high-definition video conferencing product that is one of the most advanced solutions in the collaboration technology space. TelePresence seats participants from various locations at a lifelike virtual conference table, made up of each person's local table and a series of large, high-definition display screens. Participants physically sit in identical, specially designed rooms where even the paint, chairs, and background art match, to further foster the illusion that they are truly sitting face to face in one room.

Cisco's TelePresence is about as personal and life-like as virtual communication can get without the participants being physically together. As for many solutions that require customers to change what they believe or how they do things, it is hard to describe with just words or photographs. Knowing that seeing it is believing it and understanding it, Cisco uses the product to sell the product.

To help its potential customers envision their "virtual reality" of using TelePresence to solve their need for effective virtual interaction, Cisco makes heavy use of video programming to show the solution in action as it is being described. At the TelePresence web site (http://www.cisco.com/telepresence), visitors can view videos about the technology behind the solution, about the implementation process, about how to rent Cisco's public rooms rather than invest to build your own, and many other topics. These online efforts are terrific for customers entering the TRY step: prospects "pull" based on their needs, with easy ways to visualize their virtual work needs being solved.

Cisco cleverly placed its TelePresence solution on TV prime time. I caught the United States president and three other world leaders using it to hold an urgent meeting in Fox's 2008 fictional movie 24: Redemption, a spin-off of the popular drama series 24.

Serious potential customers (deeper into the TRY step) can tour the rooms at Cisco offices and see them in action. Some rent Cisco's public rooms to hold meetings. While the rental of the rooms is a revenue-generating product for Cisco, it is also the richest possible way for Cisco to help sell the more expensive build-out of proprietary rooms around the world. Use the product to sell the product.

The *Customer* Point of View

(Mapping your target customer experience)

Exercise 4.1
Is anybody out there?

Often your target customers are not making the decision independently, but instead are either under overt influence from an authority or more covert pressures from the community. Think about your target customers as they envision putting your solution to work. From their point of view, do they need to sell their preferred solution to someone else? A colleague? Boss? Parent? Jot down who influences the buying decision in the grid on the following page.

It would be ideal—in your customer's eyes—if you could do that influencing work for them. There may be ways you could better empower your prospect to justify the choice of your solution to these influencers. What could you do for each influencer that you listed? Take notes in the second column.

Who influences your prospect?	Ways to help your prospect share with this influencer the reality they envision when they see your solution in action.
	1. 2.
	1. 2.
	1. 2.
	1. 2.

Exercise 4.2
Get emotional

Identify two or three of the most important emotions target customers should feel at the TRY step of the customer experience. By "most important," I mean those emotions that move customers furthest and fastest toward a problem solved well.

In the table on the facing page:

1) Circle the 10 emotions target prospects or customers should feel at this step of the customer experience.

2) Of the 10 words you circled, highlight the five that you believe are most important.

3) Of the five words you highlighted, place a star next to the two or three you believe are the most important at this step.

Emotions target customers should feel at the TRY step To move furthest and fastest to a choice, the most important things they should feel are:				
In control	Creative	Elite	Organized	Passionate
Curious	Excited for change	Smarter	Courageous	Trusting
Committed	Protected	Personally recognized	Heroic	Predictable
Respectful of tradition	Impressed	Responsible	Future-focused	Safe
Open	Sense of urgency	Efficient	Empowered	Innovative
Sense of achievement	Collaborative	Precise	Loyal	Optimistic
Respected	Agreeable	Happy	Surprised	Valued
Other:	Other:	Other:	Other:	Other:

Exercise 4.3
Understand your customer's decision criteria

This step of the customer experience, from your point of view, is about using your differentiators to demonstrate why you are the best choice to solve your customers' need. To win their selection, you must start with defining what must happen and how a prospect must feel—from *their* point of view—as they narrow the field.

The ideal and must-have (table stakes) events and emotions you identify are your customer experience requirements for this step.

Use the table on the facing page to map your answers.

I have included some examples from the perspective of target situations in a variety of settings to help illustrate the types of things that should appear in each box.

Your *target customer's* point of view:		Tangible elements (things I see and touch)	Intangible elements (things I sense and feel)
As I TRY this product or service, what do I want to have happen?	The <u>ideal</u>: What does "marvelous" look like? For your target customer:	*Example: Your demo site included every task I could think of to use it for; no links were broken or turned off.*	*Example: I felt trusted as you let me use the product on my own for a while.*
	The <u>table stakes</u>: What does "satisfactory" look like? For your target customer:	*Example: The salesperson knew their facts and figures.*	*Example: I felt acknowledged when I walked in the door.*
	The <u>wrong fit</u>: What does "disappointing" look like? For your target customer:	*Example: There was no way to see what the color really looks like on a wall instead of just on a computer screen.*	*Example: I felt out of place.*

Your Organization's Point of View

(Defining daily actions that unlock reward)

Exercise 4.4
Use it to sell it

Your mission: Leverage what you already have. What tangible and intangible assets do you have to demonstrate your solution and its impact on the problem you solve well? Use this exercise to collect your thoughts across five key kinds of assets; you may have other columns to add.

On the left, note the virtual reality—or vision of what problem solved well you are out to create for your target customers.

Then in each column, define how you can use your product, service and process actions to demonstrate why you are the best solution (I've included some clues to get you started).

How can you help target customers envision themselves using your product or service to solve their problem?					
The virtual reality we must create is:	SAMPLE	DEMONSTRATION	TESTIMONIAL	EXPERIMENT	INFLUENCERS

Exercise 4.5
It takes a village

If you have completed the exercises here and in the full experience map in the back of the book on pages 216 - 217, you probably have more than a few ideas about your target experience and how to use it. In most cases you will make many of the same decisions you always have, but make them from a different, customer experience point of view. Some reward takes a village—a group of like-minded people who contribute different expertise, functions and accountabilities to initiatives that re-set how things get done. The purpose of the following two-part exercise is to define and prioritize the initiatives that require a village to get your reward. You will find this same exercise at the conclusion of each chapter, for use at each step along the customer experience wheel.

Part 1

Look back at your work in this chapter. What must you *stop, change or create* to move your organization into better alignment with your target customer experience?

- *Stop:* Things your company does that are in the way, or pulling you in a direction that doesn't match your target experience
- *Change:* Things you must keep doing, but do differently
- *Create:* Things that don't exist at your company or aren't done at all—but should exist or be done

List those things in the left column. Use your instinct and existing knowledge to say whether each initiative will take a small, moderate or huge amount of time, people and money.

Be inclusive! Think across disciplines to include finance, legal, IT, HR, sales, marketing, operations and the CEO.

	Initiative to *stop, change or create* how things get done	People (Circle One)	Time (Circle One)	Money (Circle One)
❶		A FEW SOME A LOT	A LITTLE SOME A LOT	A LITTLE SOME A LOT
❷		A FEW SOME A LOT	A LITTLE SOME A LOT	A LITTLE SOME A LOT
❸		A FEW SOME A LOT	A LITTLE SOME A LOT	A LITTLE SOME A LOT
❹		A FEW SOME A LOT	A LITTLE SOME A LOT	A LITTLE SOME A LOT
❺		A FEW SOME A LOT	A LITTLE SOME A LOT	A LITTLE SOME A LOT

Part 2

Plot the actions you have listed in part 1 into the chart below, based on the estimates you made for time and effort ("doability" axis) and your estimate of the impact to financial performance reward each action will likely have ("impact" axis).

A reminder of the specific measures of performance for this step follows this exercise.

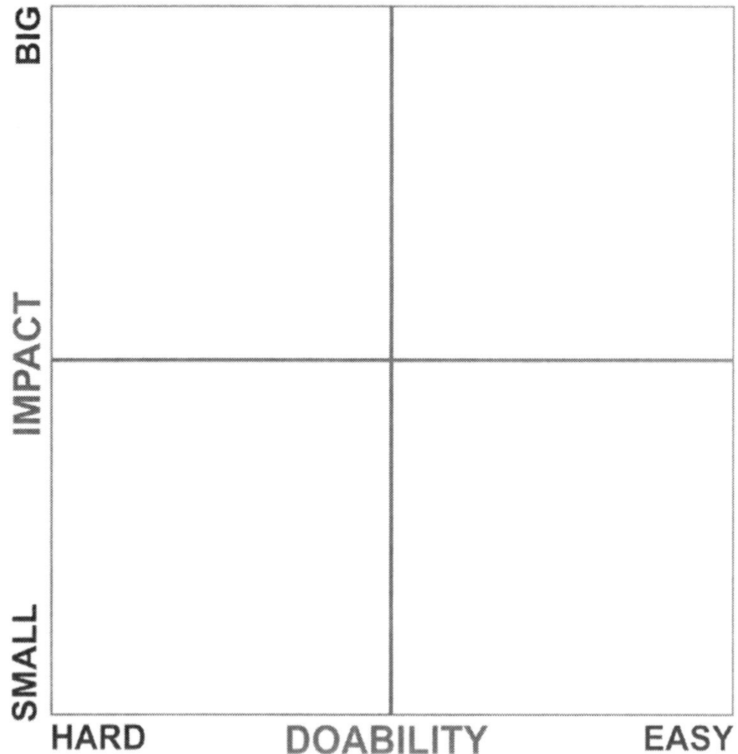

Once you have plotted your village initiatives, pick at least three (to gain traction) and no more than five (to keep things simple). Then go for it!

Key performance indicators at the TRY / DEMONSTRATE step

Is your customer experience making you money or costing you money? Here's how to arrive at the answer. Your actions' impact on business in this step will be measurable in the following operating metrics.

If you aren't monitoring these items already, you may want to start doing so, or at least take a one-time baseline measurement to help you assess your success down the line.

I have noted which metrics are leading performance indicators (those that are predictive of future success) and which are lagging (those that reactively measure performance outcomes).

Leading → Sales close ratio

Leading → Return on your total investment to acquire customers (staff, contractors and program expenses in sales, marketing and advertising)

Lagging ← Speed to close

Lagging ← Actual vs. target price position (stronger leverage to charge for your solution based on value; weaker market or buyer price pressure)

Leading → Overall customer profitability

Leading → Customer satisfaction scores—or even better, at the end of the buying process, measure the ratio of satisfied vs. captive customers

If you invest in only what contributes to solving a problem well, and serve only the target customers with that problem, your business will get and keep more customers. At this step, this means demonstrating the problem solved, not a list of features or prices. You'll make more money. You will find yourself guided by this mutual self interest at this step.

Move to the next chapter if you can confidently say these things about…

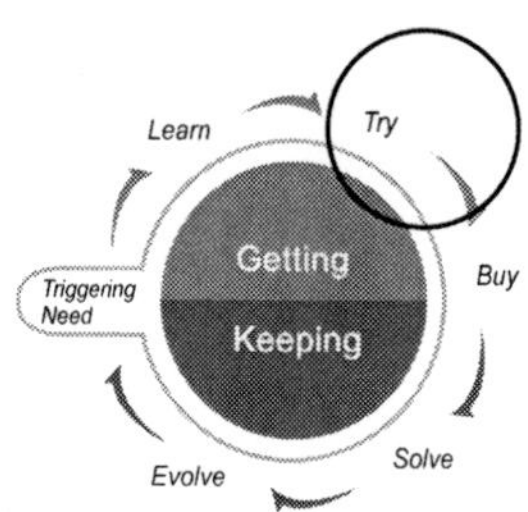

…your customer's target experience

I know what my customers want to learn, see or try out to envision their life after their problem is solved.

My customers know how my solution is different from the other options they have to solve the need.

I know who influences my customers' buying decisions. I understand what my prospects would want to show or share with those influencers.

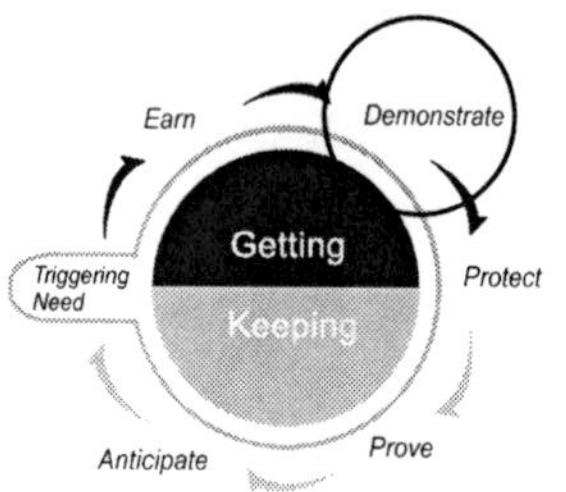

…your organization's target experience

I know what I must do to demonstrate how I solve the problem well.

I know what vocabulary my customer will use as they talk to me. I know what emotions they need to feel.

I know which criteria my target customers use to narrow their options. I know which tangible and intangible elements are expected and which are ideal.

We help our target customers share our solution with the people who will influence their decision to buy.

Chapter 5: Commitment Time

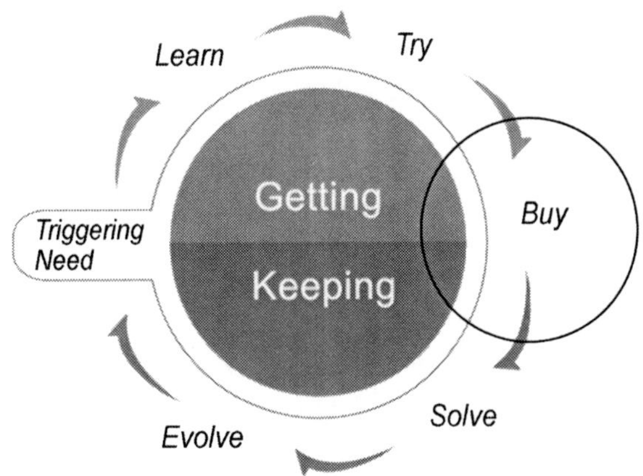

Nobody wants to be a captive customer.
(Nobody really wants to have one, either.)

"I do." No matter how emotionally attached they are to buying what you sell, there will come a time in your customer's experience when they will have to say those two little words of commitment. "I do take your product or service to be my solution, for better or worse..." The door is closed on alternatives—at least for now. This will be the prom dress she'll remember for life. Or this will be the complex enterprise-wide expense management system employees will live with for the next several years as a firm executes the CFO's vision of savings and efficiency.

Buying, at its core, is committing.

BUY:
To formalize a mutual commitment with the seller; to offer something of value in exchange for a promised solution.

This step begins when your customer makes the commitment to your solution. It ends when your customer believes he can begin to use your product or service to solve his need.

That's simple enough from your customer's point of view, but many organizations find the line that marks where this step ends to be a fuzzy one. That's because in the real world, this step ends when the customer thinks it ends.

Staying with our software installation metaphor, if the customer views installation as a process of co-creating how the solution will be put to work, then he may think the BUY step is done when he puts a pen to your contract. If he can't imagine solving anything until your last installation person leaves, then BUY ends only when your six-month software implementation is complete.

A B2B enterprise software company embarking on an implementation and a three-year service contract may feel this more acutely than, say, the cola company whose label is on the soda that just fell out of the vending machine. Yet in both cases the customer commits with time, money and perhaps even her personal reputation. To your customer, this is her commitment in exchange for your commitment. Here, commitment takes two.

From your company's perspective, you have invested much to get here: you earned your target customers' consideration, and you won their choice by demonstrating why you are best to solve their need—and you are hungry for the payoff of a purchase. In reality, your company is vulnerable here as well. You will commit with your promise, protect them with convenience and control as they buy, and affirm the great decision they made to choose you.

Your goal is to make them love their decision, to make them feel smart and affirmed. Oh yes, and take the reward payoff of their purchase.

PROTECT:

To affirm the buyer's choice; to deliver convenience, control and a sound solution in exchange for something of value.

You are out to transform your willing prospects into satisfied customers. You don't want *captive* customers, who emerge from the buying process committed but disenchanted by an argument over something in the proverbial fine print.

Satisfied customers buy more per purchase. Captive customers buy just what they feel they must to solve their problem. Satisfied customers bond to you in exchange for convenience and control. Captive customers will use your solution because they don't want to waste their money, but leave as fast as they can.

Clear choice, yes?

As in any mutual relationship, getting this step right takes attention to several things at once:

1) *Understand—and act on—your customers' notions of convenience and control.* Define "convenience" and "control" the way your customer would define them. Then align your buying process and your sales close approach to match.

2) *Use what you've learned about each customer* to keep the experience relevant and personal. Protect them from generic processes and repetitive requests for action or information. Resist the urge to let "operational efficiency" or "future marketing opportunity" distract you from your goal to shepherd this customer swiftly to a problem solved.

   Remember that your customer experience is inherently *cumulative*—we all have an expectation that the people we have been talking to will remember the things that have come up before in conversation.

3) *Reinforce their decision.* As your customers stare into your eyes and say their "I do," give them a look back that has them saying to themselves, "Wow. We agree exactly on this mutual commitment. This decision is perfect."

> Reinforcing their decision also means acknowledging when "done" happens from your customers' point of view.

Align operating actions to this well, and you will have customers who are empowered, affirmed and ready to move into solving their need—and most important, feeling not the least bit captive.

Vulnerability is an uncomfortable feeling. We have all been there. Your customers will be there every time they expose themselves to a binding commitment, fork over their money and sign on the dotted line.

And you are not off the hook, either. The exchange goes two ways, and your reputation is now on the line as your target customer proceeds to the SOLVE stage. If you are a glass-half-empty type you will see this as a gate through which you and your customer must carefully pass. Glass-half-full person? You will see this as a forceful opportunity to maximize short-term reward (such as in size of order and fewer abandoned sales) and long term performance (in cost to serve after the sale, in loyalty and number of customer advocates).

When you consider the challenges this step lobs at you, the task of correcting misalignment might not look like something you can handle with just a new sales procedure. It *shouldn't.*

These challenges demand tuned-up actions in sales, pricing, fulfillment and marketing. If you hold back at all on making changes that would create convenience and control for your customer—most do hold back—you probably have the best of reasons (ahem…excuses): legal requirements, technological limitations, resource challenges, sunk costs, vendor agreements and on and on.

Sadly, your customer doesn't care about these things. They care about getting through the Buy step and on to solving their problem.

And now the good news: It is not necessarily difficult or expensive to adjust your alignment, and it may not require dramatic movement. The exercises that follow will yield a load of "low- hanging fruit" for you to savor.

Work in this chapter if you don't have or don't like your answers to these questions:

How do your customers define "convenience" when it comes to buying your product or service? Does your buying process contribute to or detract from your customers' sense of convenience?

How do your customers define "control" when it comes to buying your product or service? Does your buying process contribute to or detract from your customers' sense of control?

How often during the buying process do you require customers to repeat information you already know about them?

Do some customers abandon you after they have demonstrated a commitment? Do you spend energy and resources on sales that are lost at the last minute?

How does your sales channel strategy match your customers' preferences for where they buy? Do you *steer* them where it's convenient for you?

Do your customers emerge from this process as satisfied (affirmed) or captive (resigned)?

To (re)define how you proceed from one choice on a short list to the ultimate chosen solution, consider the goals and actions of this step from your customers' and from your company's points of view:

Your customer's experience

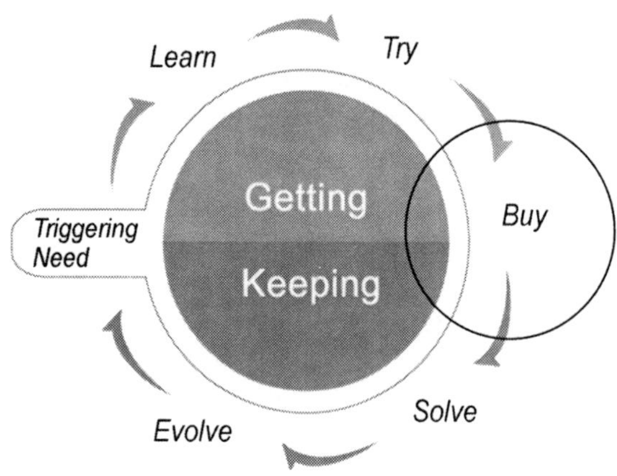

Their goal: Execute their commitment to buy. Get through this gate feeling they made a good decision.

Their actions:

- Voice or demonstrate a commitment.
- Make a choice about where and how to complete the purchase (online, in person, over the phone).
- Volunteer information (when asked, sometimes willingly).
- Offer something of value such as time, money or legal promise on a contract.
- Say "no" to or cut loose the alternatives.

Your organization's experience

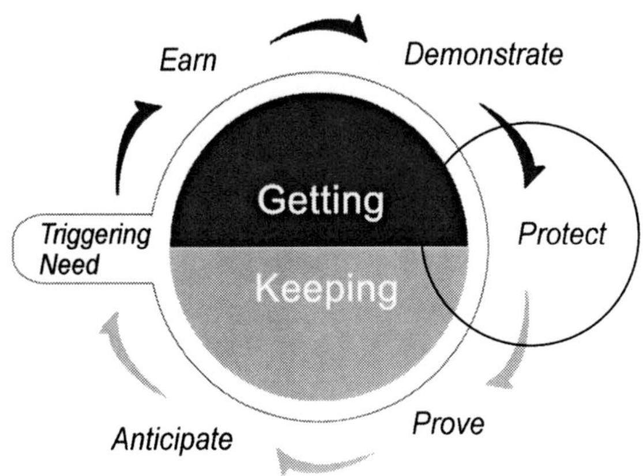

Your goal: Open the gate. Allow customers to emerge satisfied and not captive, reinforced and not vulnerable.

Your actions:

- Use what you learned in previous steps.
- Ask only for information and tasks necessary to solve the problem.
- Accept customers wherever they feel the greatest convenience and control.
- Affirm their decision.
- Allow customers to buy with appropriate convenience and control.
- Do or say something to acknowledge customers' transition from BUY to the next step.
- Measure the ratio of customers who are satisfied versus captive as they leave this step.

Use the work of others to spark your actions

This example is particularly illustrative of the work you need to do:

Mini USA: The Buyer in the Driver's Seat

As I write this book, a friend of mine is waiting for her new Mini Cooper S to be built at the factory in Oxford, England, and then shipped to the dealer in Minneapolis for delivery. While she waits, the future Mini driver is a frequent visitor to the "Owners Lounge" at MiniUSA.com, where she can track her car through the manufacturing and shipping process. (It is currently proceeding "down the Mini birth canal" at the factory, the site says.) That is one way that Mini is affirming its signature promise of quirky style, personable service and attention to detail during the buying process (which will not end for my friend, clearly, until she is driving her new car off of the lot).

More unique to Mini, however, are the other features within the Owners Lounge of the site. Soon-to-be Mini drivers can browse through lists of "idiosyncrasies" of the car style they have chosen, as described in one list by Mini marketing staff, and as described in another list by actual Mini drivers themselves.

There, drivers can start familiarizing themselves ahead of time with the features and oddities of their car—that the doors can be unlocked by pulling on the door handle once, then again to open, or that the turn signal wand returns to the center position immediately, and how hard you push it determines whether it flashes once or twice, or until a turn is complete.

This puts the Mini buyer in a good degree of control over how much "studying up" he or she does while the car winds its way through the assembly line and across the ocean. For buyers who engage in this part of the buying step, actual delivery day could be a quick in-and-out moment at the dealership. In this case the buyer feels in control and the salesperson saves time that could be better spent selling other cars. For those who prefer in-person training, pick-up time could last a while as the salesperson walks the buyer through the car's bits and bobs. In this case, the salesperson can justify the time spent satisfying the buyer, affirming their choice and delivering on the promise of attentive service.

The *Customer* Point of View
(Mapping your target customer experience)

Exercise 5.1
Start and stop

In one sentence, describe the moment at which your target customer would say he or she ceases the TRY phase and makes a firm commitment to buy from you.

____

____

In one sentence, describe the moment at which your target customer would say that the BUY process ends, the point at which he or she feels locked in and begins to use your solution to address the problem.

____

____

Now jot down a few notes about how that compares to your internal definitions of the BUY process—such as the timing of a signed contract or of your revenue recognition trigger relative to the customer's starting point.

____

____

Exercise 5.2
What do you mean by that?

Giving your buyers the convenience and control they want and deserve requires knowing how your buyers define "convenience" and "control." At one company, we asked customers why they *always* chose to buy online. Their top two answers: convenience and control. We asked another group of customers why they always chose to buy at a retail store. Their answers? You guessed it: convenience and control. For the online buyers, "convenience" meant buying at 2 a.m. in their pajamas. For the retail buyers, "convenience" was stopping by on the way home and getting what they wanted immediately.

It's your turn to define what control and convenience means *to your target customers.* Put yourself in their shoes.

Then, select the five top terms from the list below and on the following page that a customer would use to describe *convenience and control* when buying what you sell.

- ☐ I get through the purchase process quickly
- ☐ I get face-to-face service
- ☐ I feel I am building a relationship with a person within your organization
- ☐ You protect my privacy
- ☐ I get to buy where I want
- ☐ I get to choose the terms of sale
- ☐ I get to "configure" or customize my solution
- ☐ You never ask me anything I've already told you
- ☐ I get to help myself
- ☐ You help me step by step

- [ ] The technology that enables this step is really efficient
- [ ] Every step of my purchase process is crystal clear
- [ ] I get to choose my form of payment
- [ ] I have a choice in timing of payment(s) / financing options
- [ ] I get to choose delivery options
- [ ] You remind me / keep my product specs /information close at hand
- [ ] You let me lead / low-key environment
- [ ] You encourage me / proactively point out each step
- [ ] Other ________________________________
- [ ] Other ________________________________
- [ ] Other ________________________________

Now, look back at all the elements of convenience and control you have checked above.

Circle no more than three that are the pivotal keys to your success at this step.

In other words, go beyond "table stakes" or "of course!" from your customer's point of view—and define the factors that do the most to protect your customers and establish a profitable mutual commitment between you and them.

Exercise 5.3
The first thing I do is…?

Are you thinking about doing or already doing research with customers? Here is an easy way to get more from that investment.

Add three simple sets of questions to your research:

What to ask customers	Payoff for knowing this
1. What does my product or service do for you? What does it enable you to do, to have or to be?	Validation of the problem solved—grounds everything you do
2. What factors in our buying process helped you feel convenience and control?	Knowledge of what you must do to protect them as you make a mutual commitment
3. When you completed your last purchase, did you feel less sure or more confident than ever that you made a good decision?	A direct performance measure of your effectiveness at this step. An indicator that your organization's needs and actions are (or are not) in alignment with your customers' experience.

Exercise 5.4
Understand your customer's decision criteria

When going through the process of solving their need, your target customer has a mental bar. Above it they will be delighted. At it, satisfied. Below it, disappointed.

The factors that determine how well you rise to that bar at this step include both tangible and intangible elements. Think from your customer's point of view about those events. What are the things that have to happen, and what do they want to feel, assuming your solution is simply satisfactory? What about marvelous?

In the grid on the following page, jot down some statements your target customer might make from the perspective of a problem solved ideally, at a table stakes level and at an unsatisfactory level.

I have included some examples from the perspective of target situations in a variety of settings, to help illustrate the types of things that should appear in each box.

Your *target customer's* point of view:		**Tangible elements (things I see and touch)**	**Intangible elements (things I sense and feel)**
As I BUY this product or service, what do I want to have happen?	The ideal: What does "marvelous" look like? For your target customer:	*Example: The order form was simpler and faster than I am used to, and the pre-populated information was 100% correct.*	*Example: I felt trusted when you let me use the product on my own for a while.*
	The table stakes: What does "satisfactory" look like? For your target customer:	*Example: The price was clear to me.*	*Example: I felt acknowledged when I walked in the door.*
	The wrong fit: What does "disappointing" look like? For your target customer:	*Example: I stood in line forever.*	*Example: I felt out of place.*

Your Organization's Point of View

(Defining daily actions that unlock reward)

Exercise 5.5
Would you like fries with that?

The placement of cross-sell and up-sell opportunities should be aligned with the expectations your customers bring to the buying process. Translation: Your customers should *welcome* new buying opportunities, as a means to enhance the solution they have chosen to solve their need, or as a way to get to the solution faster.

How well do you do at this alignment? Start by stating where the BUY process begins and end, from your customers' point of view:

STARTS: ____

STOPS: ____

Now, in the left-hand column of the table on the next page, map out the major steps that your customer takes between those start and stop moments. (Steps might include such things as "informs me of decision," "receives terms of agreement and payment," "signs contract" or "enters credit card.")

In the middle column note each of the steps in your buying process at which you present cross-sell and up-sell opportunities.

In the right column, assess whether your up-sell activities are perceived as positively contributing to your customers' perception of convenience and control or negatively detracting from that perception of convenience and control.

Chronological steps in the buying process (from your target customer's point of view)	Your current cross-sell, up-sell or information gathering activities	Positively or negatively received? (Circle one)
1.		+ / -
2.		+ / -
3.		+ / -
4.		+ / -
5.		+ / -

Exercise 5.6
Things you do that are generic

Far too often, businesses gain vast knowledge of their customers during their LEARN and TRY experience, only to ignore that knowledge by putting every customer through a generic buying process. Think of a woman who has been trying on clothes for 20 minutes and talking with a sales person on a first-name basis the whole time, only to arrive at the counter and hear the clerk ask, "who was helping you today?"

Or even worse, think of a corporate customer who has been negotiating with a company for two weeks, finally asking for a contract and receiving a generic document with the first field requesting "NAME."

On the left side of the chart on the next page, list some of the important information you gain about your customers before they reach the BUY step. (Their name, information about their company, the way they intend to pay for their purchase, their expectation on delivery dates, their contact information.)

In the middle, indicate how necessary that information really is to your ability to deliver on your promise to solve their need or problem well.

Then, on the right side, list points in your buying process where you ask your customers to repeat that information for you, violating the "experience is cumulative" expectation your customers have.

Finally, use the box at the bottom to identify three or four ways you could quickly alter your processes to reduce that repetition.

Information you collect	How critical is this information to your success? (Circle one)	Points of repetition
	VERY SOMEWHAT LITTLE NOT AT ALL	
	VERY SOMEWHAT LITTLE NOT AT ALL	
	VERY SOMEWHAT LITTLE NOT AT ALL	
	VERY SOMEWHAT LITTLE NOT AT ALL	

A few obvious things we should do to get out of the way of our customers and reduce repetition:

1.

2.

3.

Exercise 5.7
It takes a village

If you have completed the exercises here and in the full experience map on pages 216 - 217, you probably have more than a few ideas about your target experience and how to use it. In most cases you will make many of the same decisions you always have, but make them from a different, customer experience point of view. Some reward takes a village—a group of like-minded people who contribute different expertise, functions and accountabilities to initiatives that re-set how things get done.

The purpose of the following two-part exercise is to define and prioritize the initiatives that require a village to get your reward. You will find this same exercise at the conclusion of each chapter, for use at each step along the customer experience wheel.

Part 1

Look back at your work in this chapter. What must you *stop, change or create* to move your organization into better alignment with your target customer experience?

- *Stop:* Things your company does that are in the way, or pulling you in a direction that doesn't match your target experience
- *Change:* Things you must keep doing, but do differently
- *Create:* Things that don't exist at your company or aren't done at all—but should exist or be done

List those things in the left column. Then, use your instinct and existing knowledge to say whether each initiative will take a small, moderate or huge amount of time, people and money.

Be inclusive! Think across disciplines to include finance, legal, IT, HR, sales, marketing, operations and the CEO.

	Initiative to *stop, change or create* how things get done	People (Circle One)	Time (Circle One)	Money (Circle One)
❶		A FEW SOME A LOT	A LITTLE SOME A LOT	A LITTLE SOME A LOT
❷		A FEW SOME A LOT	A LITTLE SOME A LOT	A LITTLE SOME A LOT
❸		A FEW SOME A LOT	A LITTLE SOME A LOT	A LITTLE SOME A LOT
❹		A FEW SOME A LOT	A LITTLE SOME A LOT	A LITTLE SOME A LOT
❺		A FEW SOME A LOT	A LITTLE SOME A LOT	A LITTLE SOME A LOT

Part 2

Plot the actions you have listed on the previous page into the chart below, based on the estimates you made for time and effort ("doability" axis) and your estimate of the impact to financial performance reward each action will likely have ("impact" axis).

A reminder of the specific measures of performance for this step follows this exercise.

Once you have plotted your village initiatives, pick at least three (to gain traction) and no more than five (to keep things simple). Then go for it!

Key Performance Indicators for the BUY / PROTECT step:

Is your customer experience making you money or costing you money? Here is how to arrive at the answer. Your actions' impact on business in this step will be measurable in the following operating metrics. If you aren't monitoring these items already, you may want to start doing so, or at least take a one-time baseline measurement to help you assess your success down the line.

I have noted which metrics are leading performance indicators (those that are predictive of future results) and which are lagging (those that reactively measure performance outcomes).

Leading → Close ratio—the funnel of customers who choose you to solve their need

Leading → Average order size—the size and breadth of your customers' average purchase

Leading → Share of wallet—the portion of your target customers' money spent to solve a problem that they spend with you

Leading → Retention rates for returning customers, your Buy step actions play a role in this measure

Leading → Cross-sell and up-sell metrics

Everything seems raw and visible at this step. Your customers want simply to emerge feeling they made a great decision, satisfied and looking forward to experiencing the solution to their need.

You want the performance reward that comes from satisfied customers who look forward to your solution. You also want to avoid the profit leaks that spring later on because the wrong customers chose your solution.

The interaction of tangible price, sales channel, technology and operations process steps, with intangible feelings of vulnerability and affirmation result in the ultimate mutual commitment.

When your customers' target experience is in alignment with yours at this step, the promise of performance payoff is potent indeed.

Move to the next chapter if you can confidently say these things about...

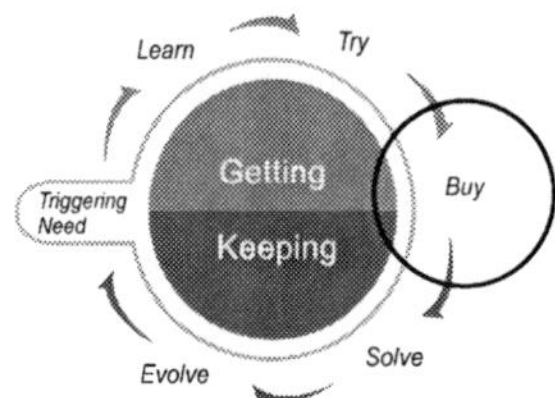

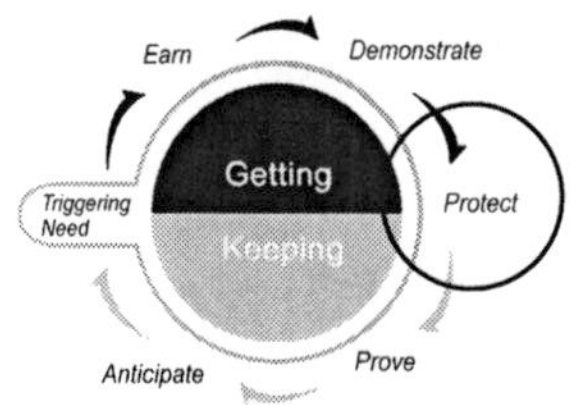

...your customer's target experience

I know what actions demonstrate my customers' commitment to buy.

For my customers to feel in control, they need: __________________________.

For my target customers, convenience means: __________________________.

When _____happens, my customers know they are ready to begin the next step.

...your organization's target experience

The ways we offer customers to buy match their preferences.

We ask customers for only information and actions that will move them toward a problem solved.

We use what we learned in previous steps here in the BUY step.

We sufficiently affirm our customers' good decision to choose us.

Chapter 6: Real Reality

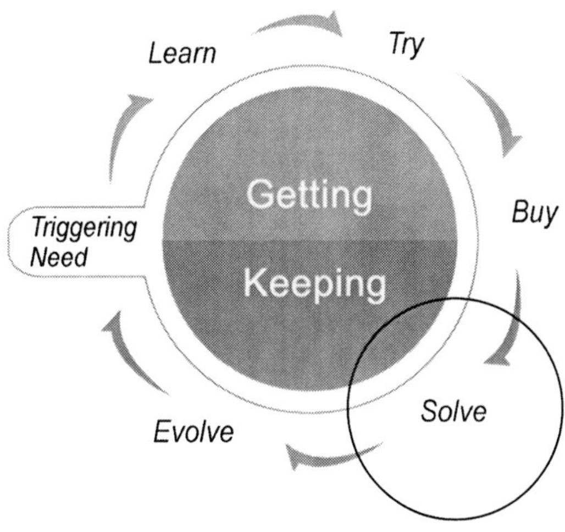

"Solved" is in the eye of the beholder. Your customer is the beholder who matters here.

Rubber, meet road. When your target customers were back in the TRY stage, it was like virtual reality—they imagined how things could change for the better once your product or service helped them solve their need. Now, that virtual reality zooms in to become the real deal. This step is about bringing to life your customers' vision of a world in which their problem is solved.

At this step, your customers have one and only one goal: Solve the problem. They are putting your product or service to work to do just that. For some (primarily consumer) problems, the time and tasks of using the product or service is quite quick and easy: imagine the toy a tired mother buys at a gas station hoping to create a quiet activity time for her kids in the back seat on her trip home. The toy either works or it doesn't—and she will know straight away.

Imagine another woman reviewing a new life insurance policy with her spouse, recognizing she had solved her need for peace of mind as she filed it away.

For others, your customer may work harder, or certainly longer. If a high-tech firm buys web-enabled collaboration tools to speed time to market for product developers on three continents, the evidence of a problem solved may take months of hard work.

If an IT director buys an electronic records management system to automate and integrate patient records across 10 hospitals in 3 cities, many months of pilot tests will pass before both medical and IT staff share an opinion about whether the integration need was solved.

In all cases, though, a problem solved is the goal.

SOLVE:
To use a product or service to satisfy a need; to apply a purchased action or item to a problem or desire.

The SOLVE step starts when your customer begins using your product or service to work out the solution to the need, problem or desire. It ends at the precise moment your customer's answer to the question "Did this solution work for you?" changes from "I don't know, it's too soon to tell," to "Let me tell you!"

In short, this step ends when your customer has formulated a point of view about two things: Your solution's effectiveness (whether or not their problem will go away), and your delivery on your promise (their perception that what you promised in all the previous steps has been proved).

From your organization's point of view, a measurable performance reward for getting the customer is in hand (you have been paid) and the hard work of *keeping* the customer—and reaping the rewards of loyalty and a larger wallet share—has begun. At this step, you must prove your value proposition is authentic, delivering exactly what you promised.

As surely as your customer has just one goal here, so do you:

PROVE:
To deliver on your promise; to validate the truth and value of the solution expected by your customers.

This requires dogged focus on solving the problem well. It does *not* mean focusing on satisfaction and then hoping, wondering or assuming you have solved the problem.

I admit it is easy to concentrate on pure satisfaction at this point. A customer who is happy after the sale is a good thing indeed, and sometimes that customer's degree of happiness is clearly visible or easy to measure. In surveys or face to face, that customer may express that happiness explicitly. But happiness is not enough.

If happiness and satisfaction are not delivered, hand in hand, with relief from the need, desire or problem that started your customer on this journey, it will fade quickly. And so will your performance reward.

Similarly, solving the problem must also ground your definition of "meeting customer expectations." While there is value in knowing if customers like the sales person, the campaign theme, or product configuration, the "expectation" that matters most is that of solving the need.

Like a doctor who sees symptoms and knows she must keep looking until she finds an underlying cause of an illness, you must keep looking, observing or asking until you know you have solved the need, problem or desire that triggered the customer's journey to you. Only with a problem solved can you be confident that you will keep customers and reap a truly *sustainable* performance reward.

From direct to indirect interaction

Your level of active involvement in the PROVE stage will vary based on the kind of problem you solve and the location at which your solution gets deployed. For example, let's say you interact directly with your customer to solve the problem— you are a surgeon who visits your patient during their post-surgical follow-up appointment, or you are a chef who stops by the table of a couple celebrating a special event in your restaurant. This direct interaction gives you real-time, rich, human feedback on your customer's perceptions of the effectiveness of your solution and the truthfulness of your promise. It also puts you and your employees at the center of the PROVE step, which can add an interesting variable to the equation. Your training, operating procedures, flexibility and personality will all be critical factors in your success.

In contrast to direct interaction, some customers take a product or service away with them—the woman with the new life insurance policy who reads through it at home to solve peace of mind, or the corporate road warrior who bought a new smart phone to stay better connected. In these cases direct human interaction takes a back seat to customers working on their own with your product.

The implications here are profound, especially on components like product design, documentation and packaging, because you won't be there in person to represent, explain, guide or ask questions.

> You must design your products, support and networking options in a way that "stays with them." This is a different twist on how to align your actions with your customers' experience, but your goal is the same: prove your promise.

You add a new chapter to your relationship with your customers each and every time they reach for, get help to use or talk about your product or service.

You may not be there for this. Your materials and your customers' peers have to work effectively on your behalf in those cases.

Finish your peas before you ask for dessert

Notice that your role here has little to do with capturing the next sale. Does that feel counterintuitive? Think of it as a case of chicken and egg, cause and effect.

Using your target experience to drive performance takes dogged focus on solving the problem and resisting the temptation to push more product. If introducing a cross-sell, up-sell or new idea moves your customer furthest and fastest toward a problem solved, then offer away. If you are so high on earning the first sale that you want another, you will most likely minimize your performance—if not at that moment, for certain over the long term.

Going for the next sale is not a bad impulse. Really. It's just premature. Remember your customers' experience is linear; they need to solve their initial need before you help them recognize the next one. (See chapter 7, where your customers share ideas and you anticipate their next need.)

What I mean is that your customers should own the decision about what steps to take in using your product or service, and in what order. Your customers decide when and whether your documentation, processes and support get used. Your customers determine when the problem is solved.

Your efforts during this step are best focused on two things: first, on aligning your SOLVE processes to your customers' choices and preferences, and second, on delivering on your promises. As your mother said, "finish your peas before you ask for dessert."

Getting things right at this step means:

1) *You understand the sequence of events your target customers follow as they apply your solution to their need.* You acknowledge that your customers' process for applying your solution will be chronological, and the sequence of events will be driven by what makes sense from their point of view.

2) *You design product, marketing, service and operations actions to match your customers' buying steps.* Whether you interact directly or indirectly, you understand what steps get your customers fastest to a problem solved. Your instruction manuals, help processes, voice mail prompts and other touch-points designed to help them through the SOLVE process should be designed in accordance with the expectations and desires the customer brings.

3) *You use what you already know about your customers.* You avoid asking your customers to repeat themselves, and you build trust that you are not putting any unnecessary burdens on the customer.

4) *You deliver on your promises made in the LEARN, TRY and BUY steps.* In those previous steps, you helped your target customer envision what life would be like once your solution was applied. Now, you prove to them that the vision you sold was realistic and honest.

5) *You know the pivotal tangible events and emotions that must occur for your target customers to consider the problem solved.* Across all of the disciplines in your organization, your systems and processes are focused on these events and emotions. Everything is designed to match the problem you solve—your help procedures, return policies, the way you set up your accounting and billing relationships, account management responsibilities and accountabilities,

and so on. As an example, within your organization, consider how the length of the gap of time between the moment the customer perceives the BUY step is over and the moment you send them the invoice for their purchase. Is that gap sensible, from your customer's point of view? Does your billing and payment process match the problem you solve, or get in the way of solving it?

6) *You use cross-sell and up-sell opportunities as a way to embellish or speed a solution.* You temper the urge to drive the customers to the next new sale.

That's a good question – or two

Here is a good question to ask yourself: How do you know you have solved your customer's problem? And here is an even better question: How does your *customer* know you have solved the problem? You will gain powerful insight by pinpointing your answers to these questions.

At a micro level, some companies may never know, exactly, the degree to which they succeed at solving the problem. The teen who wears her prom dress might consider success to be the moment she shows up at the dance and her best friend tells her she looks "hot." How will the prom dress designer know? The cyclist trying the newest brand of vitamin-enriched water might blanch at the unexpected and unwelcome sweetness of the first sip. That feedback won't necessarily reach the product managers until weeks later when sales volume trends emerge.

In the business-to-business world, or in any high-maintenance and implementation-oriented sale, it is often easier to witness your customers' feedback firsthand. Customers can be vocal with you, and they likely will be during this step, as they work toward a firm decision as to whether your solution was perfect, satisfactory, so-so or lousy.

Recall that customer experience unfolds chronologically. That's true during the SOLVE step as much as during the others.

> Psychologically, your customer is putting one foot in front of the other as your solution gets applied.

Consider any popular techno-gadget. A customer opens the box. She unpacks the contents and lays them out on the floor. Reads the "quick start" instructions. Inserts the batteries and pushes the "on" button. Reads the instructions again (and this time pays more focused attention). She then, perhaps, explores the gadget's features on her own by pressing buttons and learning from the results. Or maybe instead she studies diligently through the features guide one page at a time. She sets the instructions aside. Throws some of the package contents away, keeps other parts, files away the warranty information. And then, she puts the gadget to use.

Knowing that the problem is solved only when she says it is, the manufacturer of this gadget can consider these steps to improve both the speed and the effectiveness of this customer experience.

How do you stay with them when you can't be there?

Your challenge is, how do you design your delivery and implementation activities to stay with that customer? What does that customer want from you at this stage? Does she want reminders and tips sent daily by email? Does she expect a live person on the phone, or someone willing to make house calls to help with installation? Is she purely a transactional customer who simply wants to be left alone for a while? The customer's point of view should drive your decisions, your documentation, your service strategy.

Some organizations may say the fun starts here. So might some customers. It should not surprise you that the ones who find this fun are more likely the ones who can honestly say that their activities at the SOLVE step are aligned to their target customers' point of view.

Work in this chapter if you don't have or don't like your answers to these questions:

How does your company know a customer's problem was solved? How does your *customer* know?

Are you satisfied with your return on investment in service operations? Your operating margin?

Do customers say that you fulfill exactly what was sold?

What promises do you make during the LEARN, TRY and BUY steps that are well proved as customers use your product or service? What promises go unfulfilled, and why?

What is the most likely sequence of steps your customer follows when applying your solution to solve the problem? How well do your operating actions across the company align with your customer's preferred sequence of events?

Which comes first: validation that you have solved the customer's problem, or an offer to buy the next product?

How would your customers describe the return they get on their investment in your product or service?

To (re)define how you prove the promise of a problem solved well, consider the goals and actions of this step from your customers' and from your company's points of view:

Your customer's experience

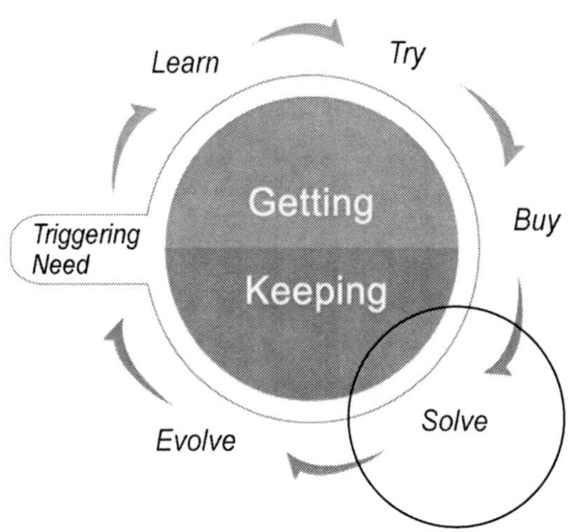

Their goal: Solve the problem.

Their actions:

- Do what comes naturally to put the product or service to work.
- Reach out for help as many times as necessary.
- Solve the problem.
- Recognize if the problem was solved—or not.
- Formulate a conscious or subconscious opinion on whether your product, brand and company can prove your promise to solve a problem better than any other option.

Your organization's experience

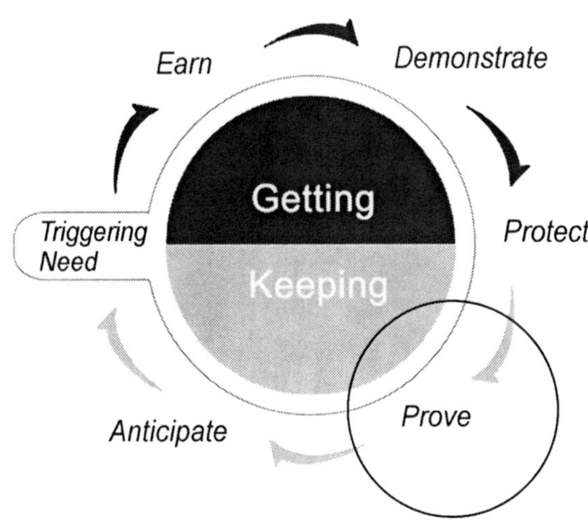

Your goal: Deliver on your promises.

Your actions:

- Learn what your customers do (and in what sequence) to apply your solution.
- Design your product, fulfillment, support and marketing actions to align with the customers' preferred sequence of events.
- Use what you already know about your customers to optimize effort for you and for them.
- Follow up to see if the problem was solved.
- Measure problems solved, customer retention and operating margin.

Use the work of others to spark your actions

These examples are particularly illustrative of the work you need to do:

Starbucks: Getting it right, again

Before Starbucks burst out of Seattle in the 1990s, America knew of two locations where they spent the majority of their time: home and work. Meetings, lounge time and the act of drinking a daily coffee tended to happen in one or in the other. But then Starbucks' Chairman and CEO Howard Schultz visited Milan and saw its culture working, lounging and filling their cups in vibrant espresso bars. He saw a "third space" that complemented work and home, and he brought it home to the U.S. You don't have to be a Starbucks regular to know that Schultz succeeded in creating that third space experience effectively for his customers. In thousands of locations, people found themselves going not just once, but four or five times a week, spending great time—and money—to drink expensive but delightful beverages in a hip environment. Those plush purple chairs, the bold smell of coffee as soon as you walked in, the gourmet sweets, baristas who knew what they were doing: They delivered on a promise. Starbucks found a pent up demand that it was uniquely well suited to solve, and then solved it.

But if you picked up a newspaper in early 2008, you know that Starbucks fell off track. The past year, Schultz publicly stated that Starbucks was slipping on its delivery of the promise it set out to fulfill. He expressed concern that the addition of elements meant to speed up service (automated espresso machines, the use of pre-packaged coffee grounds) were working against the identity Starbucks' third space customers were coming for.

And then he did something drastic: In February 2008, he closed all of Starbucks' 7,100 locations for three hours one evening, to energize and re-train more than 100,000 employees in the art of espresso and the mission of Starbucks.

While painful for the company, this event was a beautiful illustration of a CEO who understood the financial reward of aligning operating actions to a customer experience. He recognized that Starbucks was no longer proving that it would deliver on the promise it was selling. So he stopped to re-align the business.

Dell: Steering away from the road to "Hell"

In 2005, Dell made a decision to shut down its customer care message boards, the online forums where consumers could talk to each other about their challenges and ideas for using and troubleshooting Dell products. Presumably, Dell had a logical reason for this action, perhaps to reduce the visibility of negative comments or to better control the quality and accuracy of advice and information being communicated. In any case, the move backfired, as several vocal critics moved their complaints—including a new one about Dell's unwillingness to offer customer message boards—to even *less* controllable and more visible online sources.

At the forefront of the movement was journalist Jeff Jarvis, who published a series of posts called "Dell Hell" on his highly popular blog *BuzzMachine.* Day after day he vilified Dell's decision to remove the message boards and blasted the company for other customer service problems. The media caught on. So did Dell customers. Dell was forced to acknowledge that by trying to turn down the volume of its detractors' voices, it had instead amplified them.

So Dell brought back its community board in a new way. Called "Community Pulse," the forum allows users to post questions and complaints, tagged with a color-coded "tone" (compliments in green, comments in yellow, complaints in red). But unlike the previous message-board situation, where customers could respond to their peers' postings, Dell employees now oversee and post the responses. The format allows customers to see the collective mindset of their peers (as in, "there are a lot of red lines today!") but allows Dell to maintain some control over the conversation. I believe Dell is learning that although customers use its products and services to solve needs on their own, the company should remain active in the conversation in a positive way. Find Dell's Community Pulse at http://communitypulse.direct2dell.com.

The *Customer* Point of View
(Mapping your target customer experience)

Exercise 6.1
Problem Solved

Quick! In one or two sentences, answer the question "when is the problem solved?" from the point of view of:

Your target customer:

Your organization:

Do they match?

Exercise 6.2
Alternate exercise: Problem Solved

How easy is it for you to envision the moment when your customer knows the problem has been solved? You may be lucky to see it on your customer's face a moment after the BUY step is complete (imagine the *"yum"* expression of joy on a 5-year-old boy after the first lick of an ice cream cone, and the grateful smile on his mom's face as she sees him happily occupied). For most organizations, pinpointing this moment is not so easy. You may not be in direct interaction with the customer when it occurs, but the impact of this moment on your performance reward or punishment is direct indeed.

Define the moment your customer knows their problem is solved. I've included a couple of examples here to get your juices flowing.

Problem, need or desire to be solved	What happens the moment the problem is solved	What they feel at that moment
I want peace of mind that my loved ones are protected if something happens.	I review my new life insurance policy with my spouse and then file it away.	Relief In control
We need to increase our products' speed to market.	Contributors in five locations complete a live ideation session on our new collaboration tool.	Productive Excited Competitive
PROBLEM YOU SOLVE HERE	YOUR CUSTOMERS' *SOLVE* MOMENT	HOW THEY FEEL
ANOTHER PROBLEM YOU SOLVE HERE	YOUR CUSTOMERS' *SOLVE* MOMENT	HOW THEY FEEL

Exercise 6.3
Let your customers show you how they solve their need

Asking customers to tell you what problem you help them solve may not always work. Perhaps you do not have the money, time or access to ask them. And since you are in the back seat now, with your customer in the front driving how your product or service is put to work, simply *observing* might be the most potent lesson you can get.

Spend a day observing your target customers using your product or service. If you sell prom dresses to solve a desire for the most awesome night ever, hang out wherever she "makes an entrance" at the dance. If you lease equipment to hospitals to solve a need to improve working capital for a community hospital, ask a client to let you observe how she pulls her data together for the quarter or during budget planning.

Your goal is to collect insight about what happens and how customers feel as they use your product or service to solve their needs. Use the following page to choose what to look for and why.

Watch for this while observing your customer	Payoff
What does the product or service do for that customer?	Validation of the problem you solve
Do they have questions or need help? For what and to whom do they reach?	Insight into trouble spots, and opportunities to help customers solve needs when you are not there
What words do they use with peers or friends? Speed? Looks? Cost? Trust? Ease or difficulty?	Insight into tangible and emotional factors that contribute most to solving the need, and their description of "problem solved" (or not)
What alternatives do they still talk about, reach for, use?	An estimate of the share of wallet you own. An idea of how well (or completely) you have helped them solve their need
If they reached for help, what triggered it, and what did they do first?	More about how well or completely you solve a need. See opportunities to improve your cost to serve customers

Exercise 6.4
The good, the bad and the so-so

When delivering your solution to meet your customers' needs, be aware of the mental bar they bring to the experience. If you perform above it they will be delighted. At it, satisfied. Below it, disappointed. The factors that determine how well you rise to that bar at this step include both tangible and intangible elements.

Think from your customers' point of view about those tangible and intangible events. What are the things that have to happen, and what do they want to feel, assuming your solution is simply satisfactory? What about marvelous?

In the grid on the following page, jot down some statements your target customers might make when their problem or need is solved ideally, at a table stakes level and at an unsatisfactory level.

I have included some examples from the perspective of target situations in a variety of settings, to help illustrate the types of things that should appear in each box.

<table>
<tr><th colspan="2">Your target customer's point of view:</th><th>Tangible elements (things I see and touch)</th><th>Intangible elements (things I sense and feel)</th></tr>
<tr><td rowspan="3">As I use your solution to SOLVE my problem, what do I want to have happen?</td><td>The <u>ideal</u>: What does "marvelous" look like?</td><td>Example: The implementation went exactly on schedule, and the communication to our employees was superbly executed.</td><td>Example: I felt proud to walk out and was so excited to show my friends.</td></tr>
<tr><td>The <u>table stakes</u>: What does "satisfactory" look like?</td><td>Example: I was able to assemble the product without help or too much hassle.</td><td>Example: I feel invited to call if I have concerns while I await delivery.</td></tr>
<tr><td>The <u>wrong fit:</u> What does "disappointing" look like?</td><td>Example: The motor is much less powerful than I expected.</td><td>Example: I'm jealous of the one my friend chose; I wish I'd bought that one instead.</td></tr>
</table>

Exercise 6.5
Your quick start guide

In your absence, your documentation has to speak loudly on your behalf. Is it saying the right things? Take your materials on a test drive by assessing how each component aligns to the individual steps that your buyer goes through in using your product or service.

We have filled in the row and column headers of the product and service tables on the following pages with a generic sample of buyer actions and seller materials—**adapt the headers and rows as needed to reflect your solution and your customer's SOLVE process.** In each box, give yourself a score.

Make notes on what adjustments you might make to the materials to better align to the items that don't merit a 1 or 2.

SCORING: 1= Excellent 2= Good 3 = Inadequate 4= Poor				
	Packaging	Quick-start Guide	Full instructions	Diagrams
Understand a logical order to get it working				
Assess whether I have all the tools I need				
Put the pieces together				
Turn it on				
See it work				
Troubleshoot an issue				
Start diving deeper into capabilities				

Chart continued on following page…

SCORING: 1= Excellent 2= Good 3 = Inadequate 4= Poor				
	Packaging	Quick-start Guide	Full instructions	Diagrams
Configure or customize				
Decide to pursue help or send feedback				

Your Organization's Point of View

(Defining daily actions that unlock reward)

Exercise 6.6
How do I contribute?

At this point, you're clear about the problem or desire you're out to solve for your customer, and you have won both their commitment and their energy to get started. It's easy to say everyone in your organization plays a part in proving your promise, but exactly *how?* In other words, how does each area or group or individual in your company contribute to helping your customer solve their need?

Part 1

Use the table on the next page. Think about the problem you are out to solve and the things you promised before the sale as your litmus test, and then identify the most important things each group in your company should contribute.

You can use the list you generate as fodder for the second part of this exercise, which will ask you to name specific actions your organization could take immediately to enhance your performance.

The problem we want to prove we can solve for our target customers:

Top tangible (product, feature, process) things that we promised that differentiate us from others	Top intangible (emotional) things that we promised that differentiate us from others
1.	1.
2.	2.

Part 2

Specific objectives and actions each area in our organization must take:
Product or service design For the things we sell, what are the features, attributes and capabilities that are pivotal to proving our promise?
Channels through which we sell What interaction is most important in each sales channel we use? How is it different by channel (for example, online, direct sales, indirect sales and distribution partners)?
Operations Consider process speed, predictability, flexibility and reliability elements that are pivotal to proving our promise.

Chart continued on following page…

Marketing
What tactics allow us to learn if the customer is solving their need with our product or service? Are we distributing what we learn internally?

Talent & Culture
What core capabilities and values must be shared across our employees? What criteria must we measure to demonstrate contribution to solving problems for customers?

Exercise 6.7
It takes a village

If you have completed the exercises here and in the full experience map on pages 216 - 217, you probably have more than a few ideas about your target experience and how to use it. In most cases you will make many of the same decisions you always have, but make them from a different, customer experience point of view. Some reward takes a village—a group of like-minded people who contribute different expertise, functions and accountabilities to initiatives that re-set how things get done.

The purpose of the following two-part exercise is to define and prioritize the initiatives that require a village to get your reward. You will find this same exercise at the conclusion of each chapter, for use at each step along the customer experience wheel.

Part 1

Look back at your work in this chapter. What must you *stop, change or create* to move your organization into better alignment with your target customer experience?

- *Stop:* Things your company does that are in the way, or pulling you in a direction that doesn't match your target experience
- *Change:* Things you must keep doing, but do differently
- *Create:* Things that don't exist at your company or aren't done at all—but should exist or be done

List those things in the left column. Then, use your instinct and existing knowledge to say whether each initiative will take a small, moderate or huge amount of time, people and money.

Be inclusive! Think across disciplines to include finance, legal, IT, HR, sales, marketing, operations and the CEO.

	Initiative to *stop, change or create* how things get done	Teams/People (Circle One)	Time (Circle One)	Money (Circle One)
❶		A FEW SOME A LOT	A LITTLE SOME A LOT	A LITTLE SOME A LOT
❷		A FEW SOME A LOT	A LITTLE SOME A LOT	A LITTLE SOME A LOT
❸		A FEW SOME A LOT	A LITTLE SOME A LOT	A LITTLE SOME A LOT
❹		A FEW SOME A LOT	A LITTLE SOME A LOT	A LITTLE SOME A LOT
❺		A FEW SOME A LOT	A LITTLE SOME A LOT	A LITTLE SOME A LOT

Part 2

Plot the actions you have listed on the previous page into the chart below, based on the estimates you made for time and effort ("doability" axis) and your estimate of the impact to financial performance reward each action will likely have ("impact" axis).

A reminder of the specific measures of performance for this step follows this exercise.

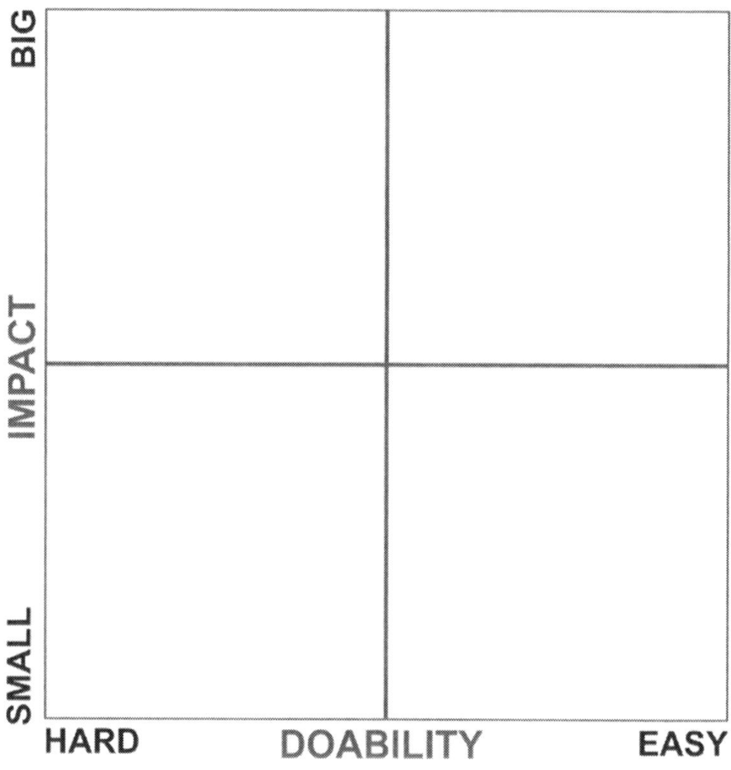

Once you have plotted your village initiatives, pick at least three (to gain traction) and no more than five (to keep things simple). Then go for it!

Key Performance Indicators for the SOLVE/PROVE step:

Is your customer experience making you money or costing you money? Here is how to arrive at the answer. Your actions' impact on business in this step will be measurable in the following operating metrics. If you aren't monitoring these items already, you may want to start doing so, or at least take a one-time baseline measurement to help you assess your success down the line.

I have noted which metrics are leading performance indicators (those that are predictive of future success) and which are lagging (those that reactively measure performance outcomes).

Leading → Customer satisfaction or loyalty scores

Leading → Share of wallet—the portion of your customers' problem-solving money spent with you over time

Leading → Retention rates—your success at this step plays a primary role in this measure

Lagging ← Overall operating margin—a good ratio indicates strong alignment between your operating actions and the value customers ascribe to your solution

Lagging ← Cost to serve (total service and support cost)—and ratio of cost to serve / total revenue

Lagging ← Customer engagement—measured in usage or penetration or compliance or enrollment, indicates how important your solution is to your customer

You could say the SOLVE / PROVE step is your destiny playing out before you. This step of the customer's experience is the well-earned culmination of all your hard work. Someone is using your solution to solve the very problem that you exist explicitly to solve well. You can celebrate, enjoy and let the customer take the reins—but whatever you do, do not abdicate the responsibility for solving the problem or delivering on the promises you made to get here.

Instead, grasp the opportunity to learn how your solution is used and how effectively it meets the need. Follow through to ensure the customer considers the need met. Stick with them here. Stickiness will be your reward.

Move to the next chapter if you can declare the following about...

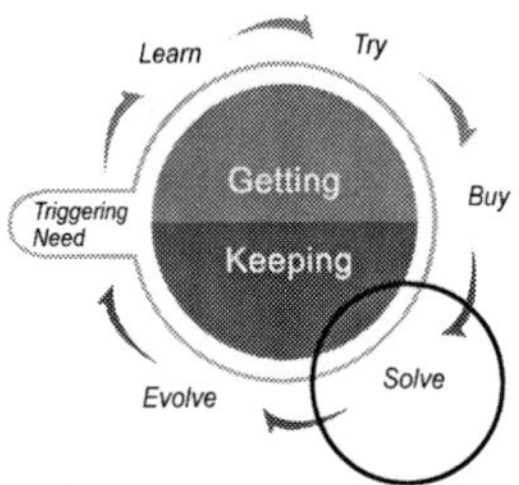

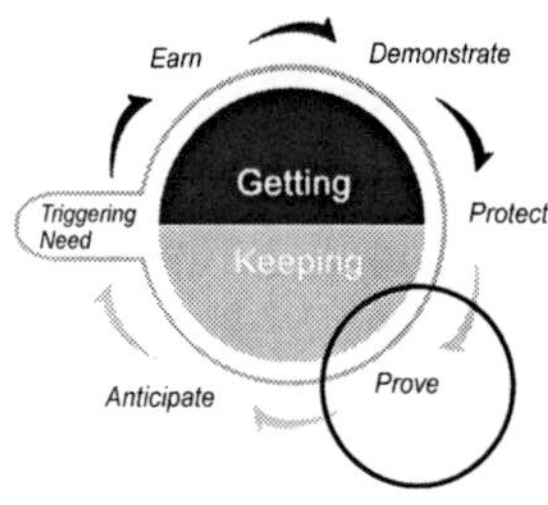

...your customer's target experience

I know what "solved" looks like.

When my target customers' problem has been solved, they will feel ______. If it is solved particularly well, they will feel ______.

My customers feel in control of the sequence of events they go through to deploy this solution.

Their return on investment on this purchase is fair.

I have a solid opinion on how well this solution solved the problem.

...your organization's target experience

We deliver on our promises.

We know specifically what "solved" looks like to our customers and how they feel when it is complete.

Documentation and service/support align well to the steps our customers take to use our product.

Our offers for repeat sales or new purchases are appropriately timed.

Chapter 7: Big Wheel Keep on Turnin'

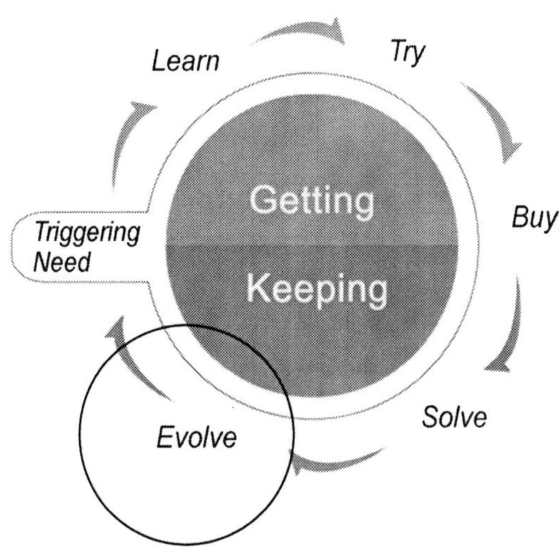

You're either with them, or you're against them.

As your customers enter the aftermath of their problem solved (or not solved, as the case may be), their role in their unfolding experience becomes less of a task and more of a compulsion. They now have an opinion about whether their need was met by your solution, and how well, and they likely will sound off about it to family and friends, to coworkers, to the media, to total strangers. Maybe even to you. They start moving past the need or desire that triggered this experience by sharing the end of the story from their point of view.

Some will use words to share what they think. There is the guy who vilifies a certain airline by name on his blog because of a flight delay last Thursday morning, or the mid-level manager who proudly reports to his peers and executives that his division's product launch cycle has been cut in half thanks to that new collaboration software he had championed and implemented. Others will share how they feel less through words and more through their actions. Think of the woman who returns four of the five things she ordered from a shoe Web site she has been buying from without remorse for years, or the investment client who registered early and was first to arrive for her broker's semiannual client educational seminar. One way or another your customers will follow the basic human compulsion to share whether they got what they wanted. At this step, your business—like every business on earth—has vocal advocates and equally vocal detractors.

They are either with you or against you.

Then, consciously or subconsciously, they start to move on. Once your customers' need or problem is solved (or, perhaps, not solved), they will develop a new need. Forever changed by what has happened and how they have felt throughout this experience, they—and their needs—evolve.

EVOLVE:
To share or reveal how a need was solved, while undergoing change or growth toward next need or desire.

For your customers, this step begins once they believe the problem has been solved, or once they determine that it won't be solved at all. They will share through actions or words the realization they have made, and how they feel about it. This step ends for them when they've moved on, and find themselves back at the TRIGGERING NEED step of the experience wheel.

If they feel their problem was not solved, they may launch into that initial step again with the same needs they had before, and move swiftly to the hunt for new credible options. More often, their initial problem solved—adequately or excellently—they move on by evolving to a *next* need. In either case, once through this step, the customer experience wheel turns again.

From your company's point of view, this step is all about anticipation. You have two things for which to prepare. First, you must anticipate how your customers will share or act out their ideas, creating open, inviting channels for them to use, and effective ways to capture what they say and do.

Second, your job is to anticipate the *next needs* emerging here, and get ready to solve them. Will your customers have the *same* next need in the future? Will they evolve to something similar but subtly different? Or will their next need take them farther afield, perhaps into territory that you don't necessarily consider your core competency today?

Some examples might help you envision this. Let's start with the beverage manufacturer who bottles water to supply healthy runners with the on-the-go hydration they need. Every time their target customer takes to the road, she will get thirsty. Her need will be the same.

Or consider a firm that manages meetings and events for corporations. A client that needed six large events planned end-to-end last year may realize it would benefit from assessing its vendor strategy, as it plans to double the number of people it wants to reach in the following year. It's new need? Engage twice the people in an intimate way.

In either case, you can aggregate these next needs to choose and measure future demand. The insights you gain as you anticipate your customers' evolved needs can inform your product and service development strategy, your approach to up-selling and cross-selling, and your long-term plan for sustainability.

ANTICIPATE:
To expect and capture a customer's ideas; to look for the next emerging needs that we can solve.

So the need for mutual self-interest goes both ways: You are either with them or against them, too.

The customer experience—and your organization's experience in pursuit of reward for a problem solved well—comes full circle here. In fact, your act of solving your target problem well for your target customer may be in and of itself the trigger that sets off that customer's next need. Are you prepared for that? Success at this step requires these things:

1) *You give customers a big, easy platform from which to share their ideas.* You cannot be everywhere at once, so make it easy on yourself and your customer by

building effortless ways to see and hear as much as possible. Welcome two-way conversation.

2) *You use what you learn as a clue to reveal the next problem, not as a clue of which product to sell.* Still and always, the problem you solve is more important than the product or service that you sell.

3) *You are patient enough to let customers leverage the investment they made in the current solution.* You avoid greed and impatience, so as not to push your ideal customers away by deluging them with pleas for the next sale. Your advances for new sales opportunities should be welcomed and relevant from your customers' point of view.

4) *You pay attention, mining future demand from the next needs of your* current *customers.* You may be compelled by the vision of shiny new customers in your pipeline. True, new prospects are an important factor in your overall growth strategy. But you do your organization a disservice to ignore the emerging needs of your *current* client base. Avoid the assumption that your current customers will continue to find their way back to you on their own, with the same problem or need as before. They are not immune to the process of evolution, and in their evolving needs you may find a channel for growth every bit as powerful—if not more so—than you will find among new prospects.

Stand by me

I wonder if you have experienced what I have seen happen in too many firms: the abdication of this step. Organizations run off to find more new customers, thinking the ones they have will automatically come back if their problems were solved. (Take a straw poll of your employees, especially in marketing and sales: how many spent most of today working on getting new customers instead of on finding new demand from the ones you have?)

Database marketing can be a powerful enabler for success in this step. Many firms collect and use robust data about customers' buying behaviors to predict what their target customer may desire next. Want to know what Amazon or iTunes recommends based on what you have bought? They are very happy to tell you. Often, they are startlingly correct.

The ones who get it right are the ones who enjoy payoff from their database marketing investments. Efforts that regurgitate other buyers' choices—or worse offer up the products or services you want to push for your own, internally focused reasons—can create the illusion that you are actively anticipating your customers' next needs, but that illusion will disintegrate quickly. It may even work against you if your customer sees nothing compelling or genuine among your recommendations.

Of course, when your target customer is freely expressing an opinion about your organization, your brand reputation is on display. To a watchful and customer-focused organization, this is a welcome opportunity to learn whether the opinions your customers share are consistent with what your brand promises. Brands are not created by organizations—they are built over time in the hearts and minds of their customers. Here is your chance to calibrate.

That said, your questions about your customers' connection to your brand are different than questions about whether you are properly aligning your every day operating strategy with your customer's experience. That is largely because the problem you solve is smaller than—and in the context of—your encompassing brand character.

Work in this chapter if you don't have or don't like your answers to these questions:

How many of your customers advocate for you? How many discredit you? How do you know?

Are you seeing and hearing the point of view of enough of your customers? (Are you effective in capturing what customers say and do effective?)

Have you identified measurable future demand in your customers' emerging needs?

Do you consider your customers' likely next need when presenting new or repeat purchase opportunities to them?

Are your product development, R&D and/or innovation activities driven by evolving needs of your target customers?

Is what your customers do or say about your brand promise consistent with the brand reputation you want?

Are you satisfied with your product or brand's position in the marketplace?

To (re)define how you boost performance by anticipating the next need, consider the goals and actions of this step from your customers' and from your company's points of view:

Your customer's experience

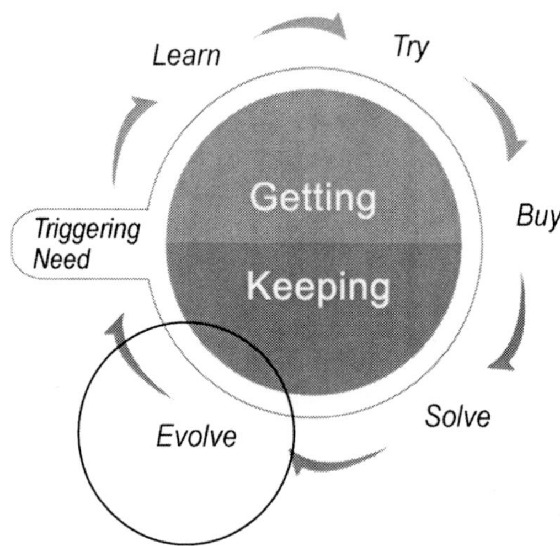

Their goal: To move on; needs will evolve over time.

Their actions:

- Talk with the people in their personal circle whose points of view they most value (friends, family, colleagues, social networks).
- (Sometimes) say something to the seller.
- Demonstrate through words or actions how they feel about the effectiveness of the solution.
- (Sometimes) do something the seller can see.
- Develop an awareness of the next need or problem.

Your organization's experience

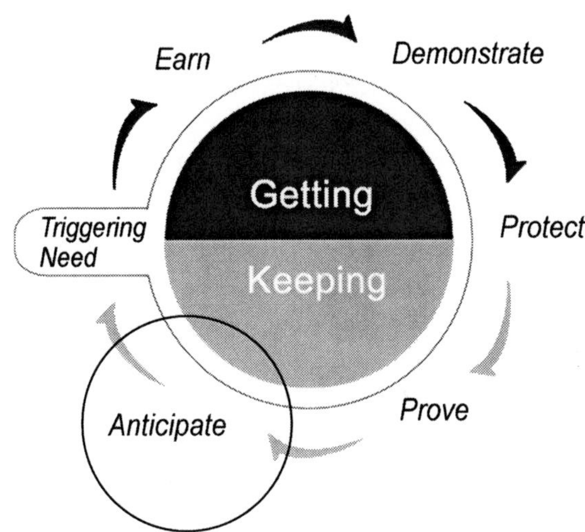

Your goal: Learn whether the customer is advocating or discrediting your solution, and anticipate the next need.

Your actions:

- Build openings to see, hear and capture customer points of view.
- Find out who is advocating for you, who is not and what those advocates and detractors say and do.
- Anticipate each customer's next need, and focus the ongoing experience on solving it.
- Determine if emerging needs are the *same or new* to the needs your company currently solved. If new, decide whether you can and should solve it.
- Aggregate customers' next needs to predict the future demand pipeline.

Use the work of others to spark your actions

These examples are particularly illustrative of the work you need to do:

Carlson Wagonlit Travel: From data to meaning

For an industry just three decades old, corporate travel management has demanded significant reinvention of its top-performing companies. Corporate travel management companies (or TMCs) like Minneapolis-based Carlson Wagonlit Travel (CWT) and New York-based American Express Business Travel have had to adapt their models several times to anticipate and solve the emerging needs of their clients.

One of these reinventions was forced by the rise of the Internet in the mid 1990s, when online travel booking Web sites exploded onto the scene. Now, instead of just offering their clients the services of knowledgeable travel agents, TMCs had to offer the efficiencies that new Web technology had introduced. Pundits predicted the Internet might kill off travel agency models. Instead, CWT had anticipated the need and built in-house its own, business-travel-appropriate version of an online booking tool. Meanwhile, anticipating that other tools would emerge, it ensured that its data and systems could integrate with third-party online booking tools as well, so clients could have an array of tools to choose from. In other words, the problem CWT existed to solve had evolved. Where before it strived to provide reliable, organized, and fiscally responsible travel booking services, now it was called upon to provide reliable, organized, fiscally responsible and *technologically efficient* travel services.

Today, online booking tools and travel counselors are both part of a typical corporate travel buyer's portfolio of services; more than two-thirds of CWT's thousands of United States clients are using both a booking tool and travel agents for their employees' business travel.

Another reinvention was required as corporate travel buyers grew more sophisticated in managing their large travel budgets. For years, TMCs had been delivering complete reporting packages to their corporate clients—reports on air, hotel, car and other spend categories broken out by division, geography, traveler, and more. Buyers knew the data was valuable, especially for budgeting and benchmarking. But as the industry matured, finance and procurement departments increasingly began asking for analysis and context. It was one thing to know a company had spent $3 million in domestic airline tickets one year. It was another thing altogether to understand that if just a fraction of that money was spent with Airline A instead of Airline B, the company could qualify for a better discount with Airline A, yielding a savings of tens of thousands of dollars per year.

CWT's response was to develop a consulting practice called the CWT Solutions Group, a team of experts in airline, hotel and ground transportation data analysis and negotiations. These analysts dive deep into a company's travel data to benchmark its contracted rates and spend against peers and industry averages, identify actions that would have the most impact on savings, and, if needed, sit at the table with the company as it negotiates with airlines and other travel suppliers for discounted rates.

While these and other trends combined to create a tumultuous industry, Carlson Wagonlit Travel has grown to become one of the two largest global TMCs in existence. Its ability to anticipate and adapt to emerging needs has ensured its ongoing relevancy and success.

Universal Hospital Services: From equipment to equipment life cycle

In 1939, a small company called Oxygen Tent Rental emerged in Minnesota to, as its name suggests, rent respiratory care equipment. Over the years the company evolved into Universal Hospital Services (UHS) as its product line grew to canvas the spectrum of medical equipment used by hospitals and other medical care centers, from defibrillators to syringe pumps to incubators for newborns. As the company aged past 60 years, it became an established provider of these products, and that's pretty much how the company marketed itself. Culturally, UHG defined itself by the products it sold.

Enter new CEO Gary Blackford in 2002. Given his financial and legal backgrounds, one might have expected Gary to retain that focus on the product line. But against that grain, Gary instead proved himself to be incredibly focused on the *problems* that Universal Hospital Services solves for its clients.

He steered the company toward a new model, in which it anticipated the full spectrum of requirements its clients experienced, and then mapped those needs to the solutions that UHS was in a solid position to solve well. The result was UHS' "Equipment Lifecycle," a cycle of four customer needs against which UHS developed a suite of solutions.

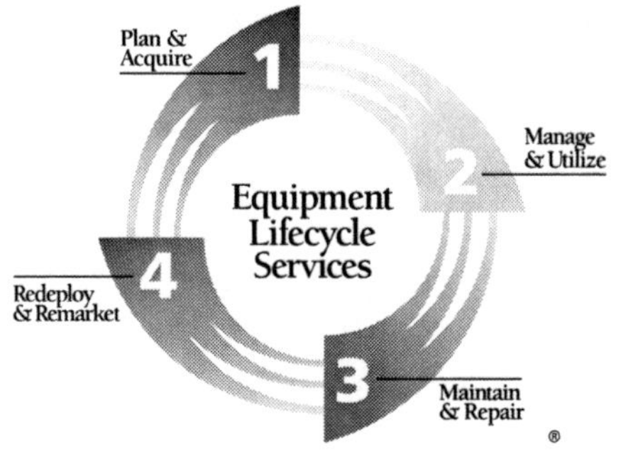

At the "plan and acquire" stage, UHS didn't just offer its equipment for rent, but offered to assist with inventory analysis and valuation, and to assess the cost of new equipment in view of the total cost of ownership throughout the Equipment Lifecycle.

At "manage and utilize," UHS realized that medical providers would see a financial value in a system to better manage the use of equipment it had on hand. UHS developed proprietary software to track, report, and analyze the use of equipment across a facility, and offered the services of a team of experts to make sense of and act on the resulting data.

At "maintain and repair," UHS anticipated the need that all clients would have for ongoing equipment service, but also a need for specialized technicians on call 24/7 - which some clients might staff on their own and others might wish to outsource. It therefore developed the capability to provide outsourced 24/7 specialists.

And finally, at "redeploy and remarket," UHS saw another consulting opportunity. Not only did its customers need to have outdated equipment removed and sold, but they also had to understand how to relinquish outdated equipment at the best possible price.

UHS consultants could walk customers through fair market value estimates, analyze manufacturer trade-in offers against re-sale and recycling options, and, of course, coordinate the deals and removal of equipment.

Exercise 7.1
The emotions of a problem solved

QUICK! Imagine your customers split into two groups: those who advocate for your product, company or brand, and those who detract from it. How does the scene look? Heavily skewed to one side? Evenly split? Do you envision a large swath of people stranded in the middle, either because they're undecided or because you simply don't know what they think?

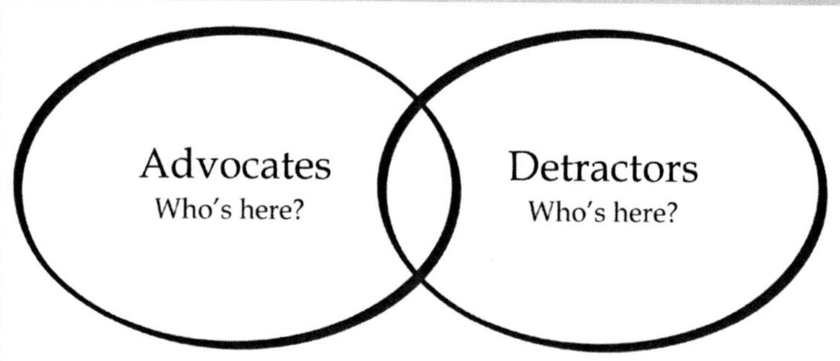

If you envision a large group of people without a strong opinion, think again. Your customers are likely not undecided, and they will tell someone what they think. (As Malcolm Gladwell pointed out in *The Tipping Point*, certain segments of the population may yearn to tell *everyone* who will listen.) If you don't know whether big chunks of your customers are advocates or detractors, you may not have the mechanisms in place to capture their point of view.

Exercise 7.2
Feedback channels

Create for yourself a virtual observation deck, where you can watch your customers as they share their opinions about you, your company, your solution and your brand with the people they chose. Imagine seeing who they talk to and through what channels. Now get it on paper. Use the following framework to assist your thinking. It might be helpful to enlarge the diagram below on a photocopier so you have room to write in the boxes.

Step 1: Begin by asking yourself for each square what channels your customers use to share their opinion. (Formal presentations? Casual chats? Blogs?) Also, rate each box with a number from 1 to 10 to indicate how vocal your customer is likely to be: score 1 for silent, 10 for yelling from the rooftops.

	I loved it!	It was okay.	I'm disappointed	I'm angry.
Friends & family				
Co-workers & colleagues				
Strangers & the public				
You & your employees				

Step 2: Stand back and look at grid on the previous page. Now ask yourself this question: Which of these boxes represent feedback that you truly *hear?* Which of the boxes reach your employees' ears and eyes? Which do you record and measure? Which have the most impact on your daily activity?

Step 3: Assess the landscape. Does a pattern emerge that suggests you need to listen more in different places? Do you seem to hear and act more on negative feedback than on positive, or vice versa? Do you fail to capture the feedback directed at an entire row? In the boxes that you didn't mark as "heard" in step 2, what channels did you jot down that might make good sources of useful information for you and your employees?

Exercise 7.3
The evolving need

The customer experience is cumulative. People naturally become the sum of their experiences, memories and lessons learned. Your target customers receive input throughout their experience cycle with you, through external and internal events and triggers. Identifying those inputs is key to envisioning where they will lead.

The following questions may help you identify what your customer sees, hears and senses during their experience with your solution. Your goal: understand then change or manage these inputs to move your customer toward a problem solved well.

Understand what your customer learns, sees and hears as the need evolves.	
1. In the course of interacting with this product or service to solve my need, I learned the following things first-hand:	*Examples:* • *I hate assembling my own furniture.* • *This reporting data takes a lot more time to sort and analyze than I thought it would.* • *My employees are adopting this software more than I expected; my earlier estimates were too conservative.* Your customers: • • •
2. While I am solving my need, and after I'm done, I will hear and see other events that will contribute to my learning. Those might include:	*Examples:* • *My neighbor's furniture came pre-assembled but it was a nightmare getting it into the house.* • *Our marketing team is asking for this data in a completely different format than what the finance team wanted.* • *Productivity is going down since we adopted this software a few months ago.* Your customers: • • •

Chart continued on following page…

3. I begin to sense that I will either need the same thing again, something slightly different, or something completely different.	*Examples:* • *I'm set for bookshelves now, but that coffee table could go and it would be nice if it matched…* • *I could use more help organizing this data.* • *Perhaps I should revisit whether this is the right software.* Your customers: • • •

Exercise 7.4
I second that emotion

As your customers interact with your products and services to solve their problem, they interact mentally with the abstract concept that is your brand.

Begin by writing down your brand to be evaluated and, in a *single sentence or phrase,* the promise you make with that brand.

Next, indicate at least four emotions and at least four adjectives that come to your customers' minds when they interact with your product and service to solve their problem. *Caution: Answer this from your target customers' point of view, not from your own.* If you don't have the information or insight you need to do this, ask a few of your target customers for help.

Then note whether each emotion matches the emotions and adjectives *you* and your employees would tie to your brand.

Do the emotions your customers experience as they solve their problem match the emotions evoked by your brand and its promise?

Your brand:

Your brand promise:

Emotions your brand evokes for customers:

Emotions customers experience as they solve their problem:

Your Organization's Point of View

(Defining daily actions that unlock reward)

Exercise 7.5
Re-calibrating the problem

What problems that you can solve well present the greatest opportunity for your growth among new and prospective customers? Beginning with the problem you solve today, and considering possible evolutions of that problem or different problems entirely, indicate in the chart on the following page the level at which you concentrate on your options. Then mark your gut reaction on whether each area of focus results in profitable customer interactions. In the last column, note the percentage of your pipeline that matches each area of focus.

Today (What we do now)			
Focus	What level of concentration? (circle one)	Is this focus profitable? (circle one)	What portion of my pipeline does it address?
Solving the same problem repeatedly	HIGH MEDIUM LOW NONE	VERY SOMEWHAT SLIGHTLY NO	________%
Solving an evolution of the problem	HIGH MEDIUM LOW NONE	VERY SOMEWHAT SLIGHTLY NO	________%
Solving a completely new problem	HIGH MEDIUM LOW NONE	VERY SOMEWHAT SLIGHTLY NO	________%

Are you satisfied with what you see in this chart? If no, try the chart again, but this time complete it with your *ideal* model:

Tomorrow (What we should move toward)			
Focus	What level of concentration? (circle one)	Is this focus profitable? (circle one)	What percentage of my pipeline does it address?
Solving the same problem repeatedly	HIGH MEDIUM LOW NONE	VERY MODERATELY SLIGHTLY NO	________%
Solving an evolution of the original problem	HIGH MEDIUM LOW NONE	VERY MODERATELY SLIGHTLY NO	________%
Solving a completely new problem	HIGH MEDIUM LOW NONE	VERY MODERATELY SLIGHTLY NO	________%

Exercise 7.6
Predictive selling

Predictive selling works well if the recommendations you make are:

- Offered, not forced
- Selective, not indiscriminate
- Focused on a problem your target customers want to solve

How do you do when presenting ideas to your customers for next purchases? Assess yourself, using the table on the following pages:

	Excellent ☐	Adequate ☐	Poor ☐
Offered, not forced	* The customer is receptive to ideas. * The timing of recommendations is ideal from my customer's point of view. * The customer can "pull" my recommendations rather than have them pushed. * The customer has easy access to recommendations if they are wanted.	* The customer is usually receptive to my ideas. * The timing of recommendations is at least decent, from my customer's point of view. * I offer the customer some control over whether to see my recommendations; some are forced. * The customer can probably find recommendations, but it may take some work.	* I do not know whether the customer is receptive to ideas, or I know they are not receptive. * I do not know how my customer feels about the timing of recommendations, or the timing is disruptive. * Ideas are presented without the customer's consent or request. * The customer must work actively to find recommendations.

	Excellent ☐	Adequate ☐	Poor ☐
Deliberate, not random	* I base my recommendations on behaviors I witness in this customer. * Ideas are rooted in statistically sound data. * I track and measure which ideas are presented to customers, to ensure ongoing refinement of my predictive model.	* Customer characteristics have some bearing on which recommendations I offer. * Ideas are based at least in part on data and/or observations of this customer and other customers. * I track and measure at least at a high level what recommendations I make, to refine my predictions.	*Recommendations are not dynamic based on any customer criteria (i.e. purchase decisions, demographic, market segment, behavior). * I do not use any past customer data to guide choices. * I do not track or measure which ideas are presented to customers.
Selective, not indiscriminate	* I narrow down recommendations to just the one or very few that are most likely relevant. * For every recommendation I make, I could (and do) offer a logical explanation for why it was included.	* I don't limit the recommendations I make every time, but I try to weed out ones that aren't a good fit. * For some recommendations I could offer a logical explanation for why it was included; I don't necessarily do so.	* I offer several recommendations in the hope that at least one of them will "stick." * I couldn't explain to a customer why a given recommendation was put forward.

Exercise 7.7
Tune up your R&D drive train

Your research & development, product design, engineering and innovation teams all thrive on a steady stream of inputs. If the stream is weak (say, awareness of your customers' emerging needs is hard to come by), designers and innovators are forced to find stronger streams they can rely on (such as cues from what competitors are doing, or the ideas being championed by your most vocal IT guy).

On the diagram on the following page, plot an X on each line under the three categories—Strategic Planning, Product/Service Design, and R&D Innovation—to indicate where you believe each team falls on the spectrum of alignment based on the inputs it uses today. The text in the middle offers examples of the types of inputs along the spectrum.

You may find it helpful to give a blank copy of this tool to the managers of each of these functional areas, and then compare your assessments. The result could lead to productive discussion about how more aligned inputs could be collected and used.

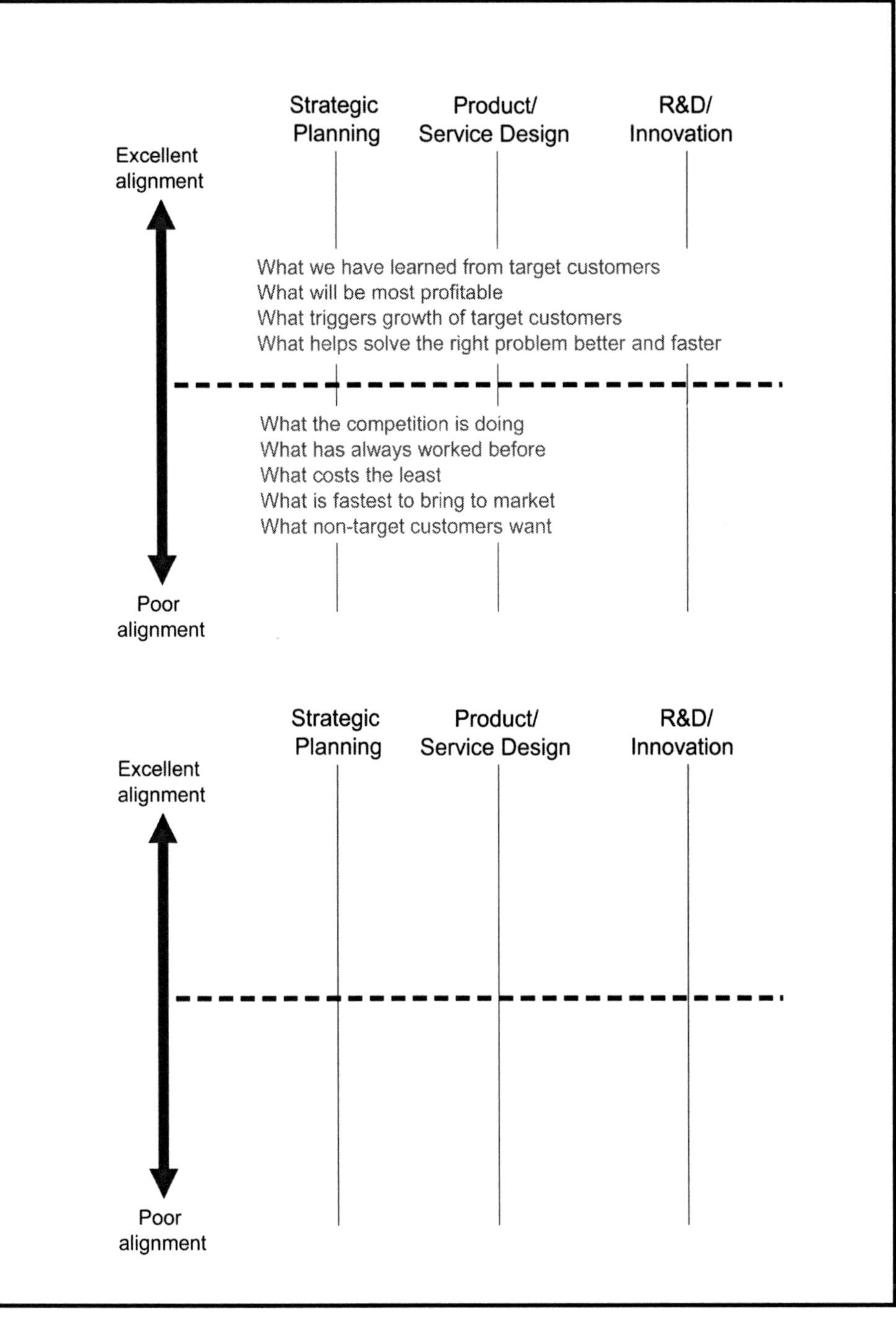
Strategic Planning
Product/ Service Design
R&D/ Innovation
Excellent alignment
What we have learned from target customers
What will be most profitable
What triggers growth of target customers
What helps solve the right problem better and faster
What the competition is doing
What has always worked before
What costs the least
What is fastest to bring to market
What non-target customers want
Poor alignment
Strategic Planning
Product/ Service Design
R&D/ Innovation
Excellent alignment
Poor alignment

Exercise 7.8
It takes a village

If you have completed the exercises here and in the full experience map on pages 216 - 217, you probably have more than a few ideas about your target experience and how to use it. In most cases you will make many of the same decisions you always have, but make them from a different, customer experience point of view. Some reward takes a village—a group of like-minded people who contribute different expertise, functions and accountabilities to initiatives that re-set how things get done.

The purpose of the following two-part exercise is to define and prioritize the initiatives that require a village to get your reward. You will find this same exercise at the conclusion of each chapter, for use at each step along the customer experience wheel.

Part 1

Look back at your work in this chapter. What must you *stop, change or create* to move your organization into better alignment with your target customer experience?

- *Stop:* Things your company does that are in the way, or pulling you in a direction that doesn't match your target experience
- *Change:* Things you must keep doing, but do differently
- *Create:* Things that don't exist at your company or aren't done at all—but should exist or be done

List those things in the left column. Then, use your instinct and existing knowledge to say whether each initiative will take a small, moderate or huge amount of time, people and money. Be inclusive! Think across disciplines to include finance, legal, IT, HR, sales, marketing, operations and the CEO.

	Initiative to *stop, change or create* how things get done	Teams/People (Circle One)	Time (Circle One)	Money (Circle One)
❶		A FEW SOME A LOT	A LITTLE SOME A LOT	A LITTLE SOME A LOT
❷		A FEW SOME A LOT	A LITTLE SOME A LOT	A LITTLE SOME A LOT
❸		A FEW SOME A LOT	A LITTLE SOME A LOT	A LITTLE SOME A LOT
❹		A FEW SOME A LOT	A LITTLE SOME A LOT	A LITTLE SOME A LOT
❺		A FEW SOME A LOT	A LITTLE SOME A LOT	A LITTLE SOME A LOT

Part 2

Plot the actions you have listed on the previous page into the chart below, based on the estimates you made for time and effort ("doability" axis) and your estimate of the impact to financial performance reward each action will likely have ("impact" axis).

A reminder of the specific measures of performance for this step follows this exercise.

Once you have plotted your village initiatives, pick at least three (to gain traction) and no more than five (to keep things simple). Then go for it!

Key performance indicators for the EVOLVE / ANTICIPATE step:

Is your customer experience making you money or costing you money? Here's how to arrive at the answer. Your actions' impact on business in this step will be measurable in the following operating metrics. If you aren't measuring these items already, you may want to start doing so, or at least take a one-time baseline measurement to help you measure your success down the line.

I have noted which measures are leading performance indicators (those that are predictive of future success) and which are lagging (those that reactively measure performance outcomes).

Lagging ← Customer retention and repeat purchase rates

Lagging ← Customer satisfaction and loyalty scores

Leading → Number/percentage of reference-willing clients

Leading → Size of the demand pipeline of new needs (emerging needs that we don't solve today, but could)

Leading → Size of the demand pipeline of *same* next needs (future demand we can predict that needs the same problems solved that we solve today)

Leading → Brand reputation

Move to the next chapter if you can confidently state the following from ...

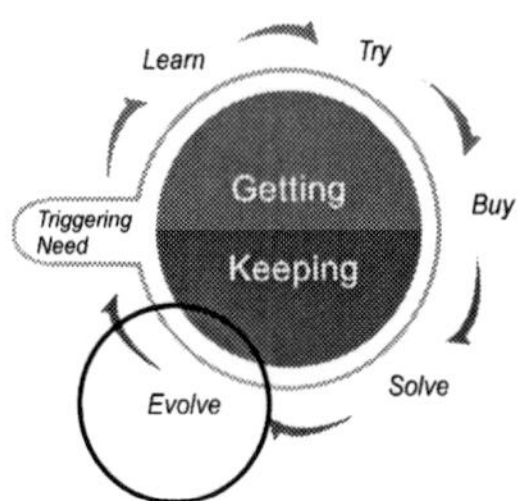

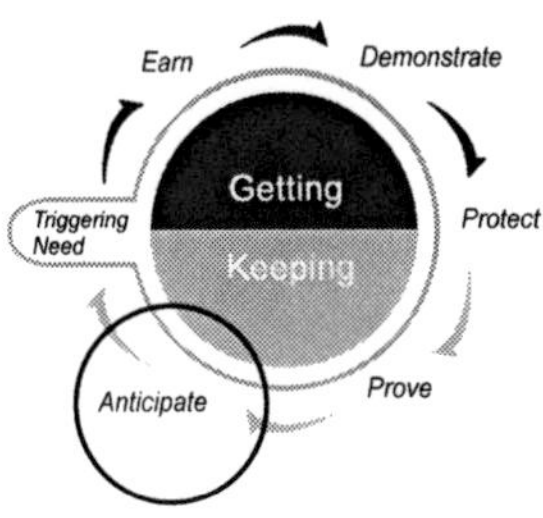

...your customer's target experience

If my customer wants to tell someone what he thinks about how well the solution worked, he understands what channels are available and feels invited to use them.

The company cares whether the problem is solved, and is thinking ahead of the customer about what he might want next.

My customer welcomes my recommendations and suggestions for future purchases, and he likes what he sees.

...your organization's target experience

I know who my advocates are. I know how to find them.

I have ample and effective channels to listen to what my customers have to say about how well I solved their problem.

I can accurately anticipate what my ideal customers might want next.

I know what evolving problems and needs I am well-equipped to solve.

Chapter 8: Unlocking Sustainability

The secret to revenue growth: doing only what customers value to solve a need.

The secret to profit growth: ditto.

So now you know. Customer experience is a key that unlocks financial rewards, not a lock that keeps you from them. In the line of falling dominos so neatly illustrated by my graduate students, now you know that your target customer experience is the "front domino" that will cause everything to fall just right and produce a financial reward.

Welcome to the next and future customer experience movement—the one sparked by the clear realization that customer experience matters because it drives financial performance. For years we've known that customer experience matters. Now we can say why.

More important, now you can address *how*. Now you have a simple definition of customer experience, and a way to map an ideal—or target experience that can be your guide. You have the principles in hand, our Customer Experience Wheel and the exercises and tools throughout this book to help you make it happen.

Your goal, starting today, is to find the way that works for your unique situation. Your mission is to make the optimal operating choices across your organization—product, service, marketing, operations, even people and investment choices—to solve your target customer's need better than anyone else. In short, your job is to get your entire organization in alignment with your target customer experience.

The secret to financial reward is matching your day-to-day activities throughout your entire organization only to what your best customers will appreciate and value. You eliminate revenue leaks caused by the white noise of trying to be all things to all people, or asking customers to do or give something that is helpful to you but not to solving their problem. You eliminate profit leaks because you won't invest time or dollars in that same white noise, because you'll focus improvement and investments only in the things that your customers will value (and pay you for).

This is not a corporate values exercise. It is not a marketing tactic. This is your operating strategy. This is your key to sustainability.

What to do now

Go forth and generate alignment! If our Customer Experience Wheel serves as a viable map for your organization, then consider deploying it widely. If you haven't already filled in the overview map on pages 216– 217 at the back of this book with notes from your work in the chapters, give it a try. This will offer you a panoramic view of your target customers' experience and your operational alignment, and cue you toward the takeaways that resonated with you most from this book's exercises. From there, the map can become an invaluable communications tool to help your employees stay focused. You may broadly distribute your defined customer experience map to your entire employee population and insist on accountability for understanding it. You may make large printouts of your completed map and hang them visibly as reminders to remain aligned.

The target experience map included here may not be your chosen format. Feel free to use or invent your own. A list may strike you as more digestible in your organization. I have seen leaders abandon a visual map, converting the lessons revealed in the mapping exercise to a simple "three key objectives" list that they broadcast throughout the company and use as the framework for ongoing internal presentations about the business' performance. Google offers a marvelous example with its list called "Ten Things Google has found to be true," and the product design interpretation called "Ten principles that contribute to a Googley user experience" which it has posted under the heading "Our Philosophy" on its Web site.

(Find the lists at http://www.google.com/corporate/tenthings.html and http://www.google.com/corporate/ux.html).

More specifically, DO THIS

If you're looking for a crisp list of most important actions to employ, do these things:

Identify your "top three." Three actionable quick wins or big ideas you can go in tomorrow and tell your boss. (Or, if you are the boss, that you can tell your team.)

Engage your whole staff. The very nature of an operating strategy means that everybody in your organization contributes to it. From product or service design questions (does this feature add to or aid the solution?) to organization structure (should customer service and sales be one function or two?) to capital investments (how will upgrading an enterprise software system enable us to solve more needs, or solve the same customer problems or desires better?), each person in your company should make decisions that move your organization closer and closer to alignment with the experience for the target customer you chose. Invite leadership from throughout your organization to try the diagnostic exercises in this book, and then get them together to compare notes. Have a brown bag lunch series for your employees to talk about the gaps the exercises reveal between where you are and what is possible, and decide how your best first actions can be translated to actions in any area. While some organizations find a "chief experience officer" to be a helpful role in the organization, not a single nit of this experience-driven performance strategy *requires* a single point-of-focus champion.

Measure and monitor the most meaningful results. Many of the business performance measures I have outlined in chapters 2 through 7 probably are—or are similar to—things you already measure. You also likely spotted a few (such as the ratio of captive to satisfied customers emerging from the BUY/PROTECT step in chapter 5) that might be new to you. In sum, these metrics help you diagnose, improve and track how your customer experience can generate a performance reward. Now take a step back and note what you're measuring that I did *not* include here. Take inventory of your metrics at the customer, product or service, brand and business levels, and decide if there are any metrics that reward the wrong things. Purge them. Keep the ones that demonstrate how many problems you solve. Your customers are already rewarding or punishing you based on how well you remain aligned to their experience—now you'll get to watch the numbers move in your favor.

Watch for worthy examples. Stories are incredibly powerful. As you go about your day as a consumer of both business and personal goods and services, pay attention to when your experience as a customer seems to come first. Look for models of greatness (and even the small, shining glimmer of a single task done very well) and bring that knowledge back to your own thinking about your organization's operating actions. Celebrate them. You'll find that industry matters little in the ability of leaders and teams to use this operating strategy to generate performance reward.

If this were easy, you'd be done by now

If this were easy, everyone would already be doing it and the playing field would be level. For proof that it is not easy, just think of the first time *today* you encountered as a consumer an experience that was less than ideal. Or better yet, think of any company, perhaps even your own, that answers "No" or "I don't know" to the question I asked at the beginning of this book: "Is your customer experience making you money?" The truth is that this is hard work. It requires discipline, tenacity and commitment.

If you are looking for a set of principles to keep you on track, this list will serve you well:

Remain focused on the problem you solve, not the product or service you sell. Practice this daily by consistently describing what you do in terms of the problem you solve. You do not shoot school photography; you capture precious moments in a child's life. You do not style hair; you make your customers feel beautiful. You do not supply temporary staffing; you help businesses keep running in times of change. Avoid getting stuck in rote discussions about how you compare to your competitors feature-by-feature. Steer the talk instead toward how you are best suited to solve the essential problem for which your organization exists.

Live the words "operating strategy." If you feel stuck, evaluate whether your efforts are extending beyond discussions about marketing tactics and customer service. Remember the lesson from the line of falling dominos: Is your target experience still the front domino for the decisions you make, or are some leaders or areas using something else (volume? profit? efficiency?) as the driver for daily actions? Return to your customer experience map and re-think how each department within your organization could work toward improved alignment in their day-to-day activity. Engage your finance, legal, IT and HR departments and not just your front-line sales, marketing and operations teams.

Purge the old. Old rules, metrics or routines that reward the wrong things should be bent, broken or simply phased out of how you think and act.

Prepare to compromise some battles. You will sometimes take two steps forward and one step back. I have met leaders who tell stories of great momentum and long-term improvement, broken by panicked demands for revenue, profit or an efficiency result of one kind or another. Your experience-driven operating strategy cannot break those laws of physics. You *will* find yourself sweating a result your shareholders or investors expect on a certain date, and your organization *will* look for the shortest route from where you stand to the specific point you need to reach. The first trick is to understand the difference between the short-term tactic—a corrective thruster—and your long-term operating strategy. The second trick is to *acknowledge* among your staff that the short-term tactic or correction is a departure from an aligned operating strategy, but only a temporary departure.

Celebrate the baby steps. You will have complex tradeoffs. You may see movement happening slowly. But this is a marathon, not a race around the block. You simply need to see your customer experience as your front domino more often each day, until eventually it becomes second nature. The closer you can come each day to aligning well to your ideal target customer experience, the more successful you will be. Small achievements can yield marvelous payoff.

Act alone if you must. In our research, we have found that organizations with isolated leaders—those who use customer experience as an operating strategy in their own departments or functions or business lines even when the organization as a whole professes to believe but fails to act—generate more reward than organizations where no one uses this operating strategy at all.

BONUS: This operating strategy works for any stakeholder group

I have focused the discussion, exercises and examples in this book on *customer* experience, but what about the other groups that have a stake in your company? There is some very good news here: this experience-driven operating strategy works for any stakeholder group.

What if you could define target *employees* and then match your organization's recruiting, compensation, culture and structure decisions to solve a desire or need for them? If your company is public, what if you defined your target *investors,* then based on the position you occupy (the need you solve) in their portfolios, you matched your operating actions to how they would ideally learn about you, try you out, invest, use their investment in your company to solve their need and evolve over time? Just as your customers reward or punish you for your attention to their point of view, these groups will do the same even though the "currency" with which they pay you is different.

Let's say you work in an organization with stakeholder groups that are sometimes at odds with one another—perhaps a hospital system with physicians, nurses and payers in addition to patients (customers). Understanding the needs you solve and the target experiences for each gives you a powerful opportunity to do two things: First, you can uncover what is in—and out of—alignment among them. Next you can build your global operating strategy on what they have in common. All in all, your organization performs better.

> How might your business be different if you segmented your customers as groups of individuals who have similar problems (or who follow common paths of interaction) rather than as groups that fall along business unit, geographical or product purchasing lines?

The last domino to fall

Imagine what could happen if your entire organization were working flawlessly as a complex machine to solve one profitable problem immensely well. Imagine every part and piece falling into graceful alignment with the natural path your best customers walk as they realize they have that essential problem, look for options, evaluate their choices, make a purchase, solve their problem and evolve to the next need. And imagine showing your leadership and shareholders the measurable improvements that follow in your performance metrics: Profitability. ROI. Cost of goods sold. Cost to serve. Growth and retention rates. Product penetration.

The organizations that have realized this vision are testaments to the financial power it contains. They enjoy a sustainable future and a mutually beneficial relationship with the customers they serve.

You need not be an expert in customer experience to see the path that stands between today and that reality. You simply need to put into every-day action the knowledge you have.

Complete alignment is an ideal. It may be something that you never attain. But the journey matters. Focus every day on that ideal and the possibility of attaining it, as a litmus test for every decision you make across your organization and you will see movement toward your goals of profitability and sustainability. You will see better performance arise from your actions.

> Place your customers' ideal experience—the one through which you solve their need better than anyone else can— as the front domino, using it as the force that drives daily decision making across your organization. The last domino to fall, consistently and ongoing, will be outstanding and sustainable financial reward.

Acknowledgements

To deliver on the promise of this book, I relied on a host of talented and smart colleagues and friends who deserve acknowledgement and thanks.

All of my fellow Aveusians share credit, not only for pushing, testing and cajoling me and for improving my thinking every day, but also for the specific roles they played in this book's creation. Cary Walski designed the cover and interior. Molly Danielson performed grammatical wizardry. After many worked on many of the exercises included in Domino, Brian Golden and Anne Davis tested every single one for relevancy, usefulness and clarity.

For all the skillful production and editing help in the world, I could not have completed this project if not for Sue Gillman and Chris LaVictoire Mahai, my business partners who were there at the conception of Domino and at every step of development along the way. Chris' calm and graceful judgment kept my thinking on track and enabled me to bring new life to the customer experience work we've shared for years. Sue was a bedrock of support and encouragement who lifted my spirit countless times. Both tirelessly carried larger client work over the past year to give me, and by extension, Domino, room to grow.

Becky Waller was an instrumental guide and translator on my journey from the vision in my head to a cohesive written work. She contributed to this book's language, shape and form. Michael Lamb of Xcel Energy, Gary Blackford of Universal Hospital Services and Jim Notarnicola of Red Mango, USA, reviewed portions of the book and were sources of inspiration, ideas and feedback.

Also helpful have been the business graduate students I have taught at St. Thomas University in Saint Paul, Minnesota have also served. And finally, I share credit with all of the business leaders I have worked with throughout my career. Our collective experience as both leaders and customers is a source of ongoing learning, context and personal reward.

Appendix: List of Exercises

Chapter 2: First Why, then What

The Customer Point of View

Chapter 3: Get in the Way (in a Nice Way)

The Customer Point of View

Your Organization's Point of View

Chapter 4: Virtual Reality

The Customer Point of View

Chapter 7: Big Wheel Keep on Turnin'

The Customer Point of View

Your Organization's Point of View

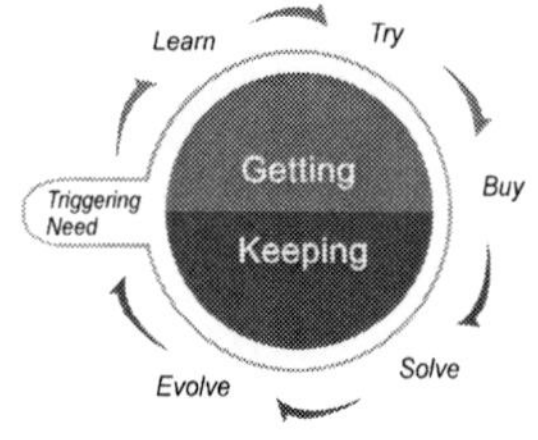

Bring your daily operating actions into alignment…

LEARN: Their goal is a short list of credible options.

THEIR ACTIONS AT THIS STEP

TRY: Their goal is to envision a solution and problem solved.

THEIR ACTIONS AT THIS STEP

BUY: Their goal is to become a customer with control and convenience.

THEIR ACTIONS AT THIS STEP

SOLVE: Their goal is to use your product or service to solve their need.

THEIR ACTIONS AT THIS STEP

EVOLVE: Their goal is to move on to their next need.

THEIR ACTIONS AT THIS STEP

…with your customer's target experience to drive performance.

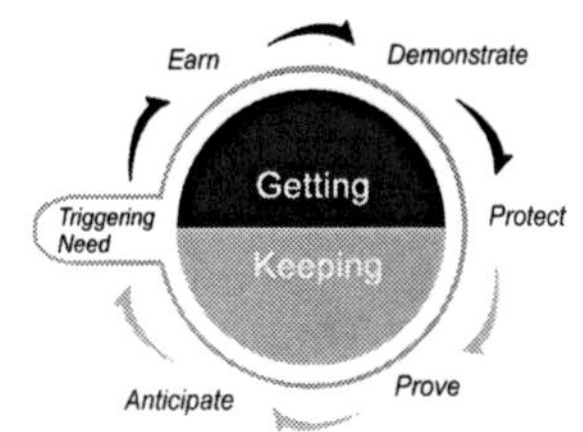

EARN: Your goal is to make their short list of options.

YOUR ACTIONS AT THIS STEP

DEMONSTRATE: Your goal is to let them experience why you are best to solve their need.

YOUR ACTIONS AT THIS STEP

PROTECT: Your goal is to protect them, affirming their decision.

YOUR ACTIONS AT THIS STEP

PROVE: Your goal is to prove your promise, ensuring their need was truly solved.

YOUR ACTIONS AT THIS STEP

ANTICIPATE: Your goal is to anticipate their next need.

YOUR ACTIONS AT THIS STEP

CPSIA information can be obtained at www.ICGtesting.com
Printed in the USA
BVOW041445260911

271771BV00003B/1/P

9 780981 930213